INSIDE THE CIA'S SECRET WAR IN JAMAICA

Casey Gane-McCalla

los angeles

Over the Edge Books

www.overtheedgebooks.com

Inside the CIA's Secret War in Jamaica/ Casey Gane-McCalla. —1st ed.
ISBN 978-1-944082-07-9 (print), ISBN 978-1-944082-08-6 (digital)

In a time of universal deceit, telling the truth is a revolutionary act.

—GEORGE ORWELL

I dedicate this book to my mother Gillian Gane, who instilled in me a passion for reading and writing, for social justice, and encouraged me to speak the truth, and to my father Clement McCalla, who passed on to me his passion and pride in the country of Jamaica.

TABLE OF CONTENTS

COAT OF ARMS FOR JAMAICA

Considered a legacy from the British with slight modifications over the years, the Jamaican coat of arms was granted to Jamaica in 1661. The original was designed by William Sancroft, then Archbishop of Canterbury.

The motto of the seal has been a matter of discussion since inception. The original motto, INDUS UNTERQUE SERVIET VNI is the Latin translation for "The two Indians will serve as one", or "Both Indies will serve together", in reference to the collective servitude of the Taino and Arawak Indians to the colonizers. The motto was replaced in 1962 with the English motto "Out of Many, One People", as tribute to the unity of the different cultural minorities inhabiting the nation. Perhaps as coincidence, the motto has the same meaning as the motto of the United States; E Pluribus Unum.

INTRODUCTION

There have been allegations of the CIA's destructive involvement in Jamaica for years. Stories of CIA-sponsored guns, drugs, and violence have been around all my life. My father is from Jamaica; I've been interested in the country for a long time. As a child, I would travel there for vacations and holidays, staying in nice neighborhoods in the capital of Kingston.

Still, from the sheltered, bourgie Kingston houses, I could clearly see that Jamaica was drastically different than the U.S. I noticed the poorly clothed children in the shantytowns living in tin houses. I noticed the policemen who, unlike American police, carried M-16 machine guns as opposed to pistols.

While driving through Kingston, I saw graffiti that also caught my eye. In many of the poor neighborhoods that we drove through, I became intrigued by simple three-letter graffiti, the initials PNP or JLP. My relatives told me that they were the political parties of the country.

I knew no one in America would write graffiti about Democrats and Republicans so I was impressed that Jamaicans took so much pride in politics. Little did I know that there was a secret war on the streets of Kingston, between supporters of the People's National Party and the Jamaican Labor Party, a conflict that had turned into a low-intensity civil war with the help of the CIA.

I first became aware of the CIA's role in Jamaica because of my interest in reggae star Bob Marley. On a tour of the Bob Marley Museum in Kingston, the tour guide showed us the bullet holes from the attempted assassination of Marley in December 1976. The tour guide claimed that Marley was shot at the direction of the CIA.

Why would the CIA want to kill a reggae singer? My grandmother bought me a book, *Marley and Me*, written by Marley's former manager Don Taylor. In the book, Taylor claimed that he was present at the execution of one of Marley's would-be assassins. Taylor said that before being killed, the gunman claimed he tried to kill Marley on the orders of the CIA and was paid with cocaine and guns.

This was not the only time I read about the CIA being involved in drugs, guns, and Jamaica. I read Gary Webb's series in the *San Jose Mercury News* and learned about the CIA's involvement in the cocaine trade to support the Contras war in Nicaragua.

In his book *The Dark Alliance*, Webb also wrote about Jamaica being exploited by the CIA in 1976; that the agency used the same tactics of manipulating the drug trade to force regime change. Webb's books opened my eyes to what type of organization the CIA really was.

The Iran-Contra affair showed how the CIA would facilitate Latin American drug dealers in order to fight Communism. I was intrigued by the government corruption. At the same time the First Lady was telling kids to *Just Say No*, the Vice President was aiding the large-scale importation of cocaine into the United States to help wage a secret war in Nicaragua and other countries.

In college, I became an amateur Bob Marley scholar and bought every album he made and every book written about him. For my senior thesis at Columbia, I wrote about Jamaica in the 1970s. My paper was titled "The Eagle, the Bear, and the Lion." The eagle was the U.S., the bear was the Soviet Union, and the lion was Bob Marley and the Rastafarian Movement. In this thesis, I wrote about how Jamaica was caught between the interests of Russia and Cuba, and how Marley saved the country by uniting the warring leaders of the PNP and the JLP, avoiding a civil war.

My father's first cousin, Trevor Rhone, wrote the epic Jamaican movie *The Harder They Come*, which told the story of a poor Jamaican man who moves from the country to Kingston to become a musician. Unable to make money from music, Ivanhoe Martin, played by reggae star Jimmy Cliff, becomes involved in the marijuana trade and a wanted outlaw.

Outlaw culture plays a big part in Jamaica. American cowboy and gangster movies were very popular in Jamaica. Unlike in America, where cowboy movies are a throwback to days of a lawless era, modern-day Jamaicans could relate to the Wild West and its outlaw heroes. Jamaicans would name themselves after the American cowboy characters and the mythical criminals of American gangster movies.

Through conversations, music, books, and newspaper articles, I became more familiar with the culture of Jamaican gangsterism and its ties to politics and the drug trade. *Shower Posse* was written by Duane Blake, the son of Vivian Blake, one of the leaders of the JLP-connected criminal organization. *Born Fi' Dead,* by white American Laurie Gunst, revealed previously untold tales from Jamaica. She told stories of politicians from both political parties and the gangsters they used as representatives, and gunmen affiliated with both political parties that later embarked on criminal careers in the U.S., Canada, and the UK.

Living in the West Indian neighborhood of Crown Heights in Brooklyn, NY, I had access to several documentaries on Jamaican history. One of the best films on Jamaica I watched was *Blood and Fire*, a BBC documentary that took its name from a speech by JLP leader Edward Seaga, who threatened political violence against his opponents.

Another documentary on Lester Lloyd "Jim Brown" Coke, Seaga's bodyguard and infamous Jamaican drug lord, would claim the CIA was arming Brown's militia of armed political gunmen. Later, an *American Gangster* episode on BET would bring up the same allegations.

I first began writing about the CIA and the Jamaican Shower Posse after the U.S. forced Jamaica to capture the son of Shower Posse leader Lester "Jim Brown" Coke, Christopher Dudus Coke, who had followed in his father's footsteps to become a drug lord himself. Given the media attention given to the case, I decided to write about the history of Jamaican Shower Posse and the hypocrisy of the United States for secretly condoning, promoting, and enabling drug dealing while openly condemning it.

In 2010, I wrote a story for *NewsOne*, a black news website, called "How the CIA Created the Jamaican Shower Posse." In the story, I explored allegations by Don Taylor, former CIA agent, Philip Agee, Gary Webb, and former Shower Posse member Cecil Connor, also known as Charles "Lil Nut" Miller.

The story quickly went viral and was reprinted on several blogs and message boards. Jamaicans, conspiracy theorists, scholars, and other journalists used the story as a point of reference, and I ranked among the top search results for the Shower Posse and CIA in Jamaica on Google.

While researching the story, I came across the name of Luis Posada Carilles. He was a drug dealer, an arms dealer, a terrorist, and a CIA agent. He fit all the criteria for a film villain, except for the fact that he worked for the CIA. Gary Webb, drawing on the research of John Cummings and Ernest Volkman, claimed that Posada was part of a CIA team of Cubans sent to Jamaica to destabilize the country and overthrow the Manley regime.

After writing the story, I came across more research material. I found several editions of *The Struggle*, a short-lived newspaper run by Jamaican left-wing activist and professor Trevor Munroe. *The Struggle* clearly had a pro-Cuban, anti-American bias and it spent a good deal of time covering accusations of the CIA's activities in Jamaica. Despite its bias, a good deal of the information provided on the CIA in Jamaica was confirmed by separate research.

In April 2013, Wikileaks released the Kissinger cables. Hundreds of cables relating to the CIA's activities in Jamaica were released. Cables from the U.S. Ambassador to Jamaica, Sumner Gerard, would cover the accusations against the CIA and the effort to cover up their involvement without admitting involvement. These cables helped give a good picture of the political climate in Jamaica in the turbulent election year of 1976.

I've decided to keep the focus of the book on the year 1976, due to the large amount of source material from both *The Struggle* and Kissinger's cables from that year. It was also the year that George H.W. Bush, who would go on to become Vice President and then President, was the director of the CIA.

My research on several of the key players in the CIA during their 1976 war in Jamaica brought me into a world of corruption and deceit, assassinations, cover-ups, and a realization that many things that were labeled a conspiracy theory, were actually American and world history.

I try to paint a clear picture of the political climate of Jamaica in the 70s. From the rhetorical battles of the politicians, to the gun battles of the ghetto residents who supported them, there was a low-level civil war in which the winner would be decided by ballots and bullets.

Jamaica would be an ideal place for the CIA to operate. Unlike other countries where the CIA would help plot military coups, civil wars, and assassinations in order to put a pro-American government in power, in Jamaica all the CIA would need to do would be to get JLP into power through the manipulation of the media, economic sabotage of the Manley government, and arms for JLP street soldiers for the secret war they were fighting against the PNP in order to win elections.

The year of 1976 began with a visit from Henry Kissinger, closely followed by riots and arson during a conference for the IMF. Later in May, Manley would declare a state of emergency in Jamaica due to outside forces destabilizing the country and an alleged plot to overthrow the government. In July, Jamaica would be a target for Cuban terrorists when an airliner bound for Cuba was bombed. Later in October, the same plane would be bombed on the way to Jamaica killing 73 people. In September, former CIA agent Philip Agee would visit Jamaica to talk about the CIA's activities in the country. At the end of the year, Jamaica's biggest star, Bob Marley would be the victim of an assassination attempt in which he was shot. The year would end with Manley being reelected Prime Minister of Jamaica.

I wrote this book because I believe in the importance of history and the disclosure of government activities on our behalf. Jamaica is far from the only country that the CIA has destabilized through guns, drugs, and other methods, but it makes for an interesting case study. Because Jamaica is an English-speaking country, a popular tourist destination, and a producer of music and culture, it draws particular attention of the world's interest.

The CIA has operated like a government-sanctioned Mafia, where illegal activities are justified by the war on Communism.

Like the Mafia, they are very secretive and very good at covering up their tracks through bribes, threats, and murder. In the case of Jamaica, when Lester "Jim Brown" Coke was finally captured and extradited to the United States, he was burned alive in his Jamaican jail cell. Who knows what the drug lord would have said would he have lived. Would he implicate his patron Edward Seaga? The man who he served as bodyguard and who led his funeral procession. Would he implicate the CIA, whom many had accused of arming and empowering him?

I intend to present a story of a country and people who were caught in the crossfire of the Cold War that became a target of America's deadliest assassins, the CIA. The story tells the roots of the cocaine trade that exploded in the 1980s, due in part to the CIA and the Latin American dictators and rebel forces they supported. I will expose patterns of CIA activity that explain how Jamaica turned into a country like many other Cold War countries: plagued by drugs, guns, and political violence.

Jamaica, a country once on pace with Singapore, was plagued by drugs, violence, and political instability, much of which was the result of CIA and American interference. From the 1972 election to the election in 1976, the murder rate would almost triple, and then triple again by the election of 1980. A good deal of the violence was politically motivated or had to deal with the drug trade. Most of these murders were executed by using weapons from America, illegally smuggled into the country.

After 1976, the illegal import of choice from Jamaica would switch from native grown marijuana to cocaine from South America. The small, politically based gangs would go on to be international drug rings operating in the U.S., the U.K., and Canada. In the CIA's attempt to destabilize the Manley government, they created a cycle of politically based drug lords, gun violence and arms dealing, poverty, and economic exploitation.

There are no heroes in this story; both sides played to win. When Manley allied himself with Fidel Castro, Seaga sought the support of the U.S.. In doing so, he accepted the help of the CIA, who would gladly destroy a country to put in place a pro-American government.

I see both Manley and Seaga as tragic figures. Manley did not want to make an enemy of the U.S.. He believed that he could maintain a friendly relationship with both Castro and the United States. Unfortunately for Manley, the CIA and their small army of anti-Castro Cubans would wage a war against anyone in any way connected to Castro. Like Marley would learn in the same year, Manley would learn that you have to pick a side.

GLOSSARY OF CHARACTERS

PNP - People's National Party

NORMAN MANLEY
A Jamaican politician and founder of the PNP. Was premiere of the country from 1959 until Jamaican independence in 1962 and the father of Prime Minister, Michael Manley.

MICHAEL MANLEY
PNP leader and Prime Minister of Jamaica from 1972-1980. Angered the USA through leftist stance and close ties to Cuba and Castro.

DK DUNCAN
A key ally to Michael Manley and a progressive leftist PNP Member Of Parliament. Closely watched by the CIA who believed he had close ties to Cuban Intelligence officers.

DUDLEY THOMPSON
Another progressive leftist ally of Michael Manley known for his pro Pan African views. He became known as an enemy of the U.S. and its policies after an argument with Henry Kissinger.

ANTHONY SPAULDING

Served as Housing Minister under Michael Manley where he established the PNP Garrison (Housing community) of Arnett Gardens. Had close ties to community leaders or Dons such as Tony Welch as well as Bob Marley.

JLP - JAMAICAN LABOR PARTY

ALEXANDER BUSTAMANTE

The founder of the JLP and the first Prime Minister of Jamaica.

EDWARD SEAGA

The leader of the JLP from 1972 and Prime Minister of Jamaica from 1980 until 1989. Was loved by the USA for his anti-Communist and pro-American stances.

PEARNEL CHARLES

A JLP politician and opponent of Michael Manley. He would be detained by the Manley government in 1976 and accused of plotting an uprising against the Government of Jamaica but later released.

PETER WHITTINGHAM

A JLP politician and pilot, who along with Pearnel Charles was detained and charged with plotting a violent overthrow of the government. He would later be arrested and charged with importing marijuana into Miami and never heard from after that.

CLAUDIE MASSOP

A Don, or community leader, in the JLP Garrison of Tivoli Gardens who ruled the area for most of the 70s. After helping organize the One Love Peace Concert with his friend Bob Marley, in 1978, he was killed by the police in 1979.

LESTER "JIM BROWN" COKE
Followed Massop as the Don of Tivoli Gardens and was a founder of The Shower Posse where he handled Jamaican operations and also served as Edward Seaga's bodyguard.

VIVIAN BLAKE
Another leader of the Shower Posse and the son of a prominent PNP politician. Blake handled the American affairs of the Shower Posse.

CECIL CONNOR AKA CHARLES "LITTLE NUT" MILLER
An associate of Blake and Coke, he would wind up testifying against them and joining the witness protection program, later admitting he was trained by and worked for the CIA.

RICHARD "STORYTELLER" MORRISON
A pilot and Shower Posse Member who worked closely with Lester Coke and Vivian Blake before being convicted on drug trafficking and racketeering charges in Miami.

THE CIA

ALLEN DULLES
Head of the CIA from 1952 until 1961, when he was fired by John F. Kennedy after the failed Bay Of Pigs invasion. He would later serve on the Warren Commission that would investigate Kennedy's death at the request of President Lyndon Johnson.

PRESCOTT BUSH

Senator from Connecticut who served from 1952 to 1963 and was close to President Lyndon Johnson and CIA Director Allen Dulles as well as an advocate for the CIA in the Senate. He is the father of former CIA Director George H.W. Bush.

E HOWARD HUNT

A CIA agent who worked closely with Allen Dulles, Hunt would later go on to work for President Nixon. He later served 33 months in jail for his involvement in the Watergate scandal and admitted to being involved in CIA plot to kill John F. Kennedy.

FRANK STURGIS

Another CIA agent who worked in Cuba and later with Hunt in the Watergate scandal. Sturgis would be implicated along with several other CIA agents by Hunt for the murder of John F. Kennedy.

GEORGE H.W. BUSH

Despite claiming that he had no involvement with the CIA before his appointment as director of the organization in 1976, many claim that Bush was a longtime agent or asset. Throughout his career as congressman, ambassador, Vice President, and President, Bush has maintained close ties to several notorious CIA agents.

TED SHACKLEY

A longtime CIA agent who worked with anti-Castro Cubans in the 60s to fight Fidel Castro. He later ran Operation Phoenix in Vietnam and was involved in the Iran-Contra scandal. Shackley was a close friend and ally of George H.W. Bush.

FELIX RODRIGUEZ

A Cuban-born CIA agent with close ties to George
H.W. Bush, Ted Shackley, and terrorists Luis Posada
and Orlando Bosch. Participated in the Bay of Pigs
invasion, the capture and murder of Che Guevara, and
the Iran-Contra scandal.

LUIS POSADA CARILLES

Another Cuban trained by the CIA. He was involved
in the Bay of Pigs invasion, implicated in the JFK
assassination, the 1976 bombing of a Cuban airplane,
the assassination of Chilean diplomat Orlando
Letelier, and Iran-Contra. Had close ties to the Mafia,
South American cocaine kingpins, CIA agent Felix
Rodriguez, and Cuban terrorist Orlando Bosch.

ORLANDO BOSCH

A Cuban-born terrorist and extortionist who was also
trained by the CIA. He was the head of the anti-Castro
Cuban terrorist group CORU that was responsible
for numerous bombing and assassinations. Like his
cohort Luis Posada, he was also implicated in the
Kennedy assassination.

THE WHISTLEBLOWERS

PHILIP AGEE

A CIA case officer who worked in Latin America before
writing a book exposing the CIA's dirty deeds and
agents across the world. Spoke in Jamaica in 1976
and revealed that eight CIA agents were working out
of the Embassy. Agee was a nemesis of CIA agent Ted
Shackley and his old boss George H.W. Bush.

JOHN STOCKWELL

Another former CIA agent-turned-whistleblower, Stockwell worked in Angola under then-CIA Director George H.W. Bush. Since leaving the agency he has spoken out against the CIA's involvement in the JFK assassination, Iran-Contra, assassinations, corruption and drug dealing.

MARITA LORENZ

An ex-lover of Fidel Castro, she admitted being part of a plot to poison him at the request of Frank Sturgis and the CIA. She later implicated Sturgis and Hunt in the plot to murder JFK.

CHAUNCEY HOLT

Another whistleblower that worked as a CIA operative with Jewish mobster Meyer Lansky. Holt would claim he was involved in a plot to kill JFK and that CIA assassins Orlando Bosch and Luis Posada were on the scene as well.

ANTONIO VECIANA

A Cuban exile and head of the anti-Castro group Alpha 66. Veciana gave an interview in 2013, claiming that the JFK assassination was planned by CIA and military officials as part of a coup d'état.

One Love Peace Concert featuring Michael Manley, Bob Marley, and Edward Seaga joined in a symbolic and ultimately a very real unity. These two political leaders had divided Jamaica into such a violent rift that the very idea of doing this concert resulted in an attempted assassination on Bob Marley's life. Surviving two gun shot wounds, Bob Marley took the stage April 22, 1978 and during "Jammin'" he called for national peace between his Rastafarian brothers.

Illustration by Beekone

HARBOR OF KINGSTON, FROM RAE'S TOWN.

Illustration of article "Cast-away in Jamaica" by W.E. Sewell,
Harper's Monthly Magazine, January 1861.

CHAPTER 1

JAMAICAN HISTORY

Now why would the CIA be involved in a small country like Jamaica? Jamaica's population is less than three million people. A country with no gold, diamonds, or oil? One reason is Jamaica's location makes it an ideal point for transport and it has always been a transshipment point for the trade routes in the Caribbean. Christopher Columbus landed in Jamaica in 1494 and began the Spanish colonization of the island, originally inhabited by the Arawak and Taino Indians.

In 1655, the English invaded Jamaica and took it from the Spanish, and soon Jamaica became a hub for pirates taking advantage of Jamaica's ideal location. Many of these pirates, such as Captain Henry Morgan and Blackbeard, raided Spanish and French ships for gold, spices, and other valuable goods. Rather than arresting the pirates, the British utilized these pirates, making Morgan Lieutenant Governor and creating what would be a long standing partnership between criminals and the government in Jamaica. The then-capital of Port Royal became a hub for government-sanctioned pirates, alcohol, and prostitutes.

A major earthquake destroyed the capital city and pirate safe haven of Port Royal in 1682 and Britain outlawed piracy in 1687, but not before creating pirate outlaw heroes out of men like Captain Henry Morgan. Later, the drug dealers would become the new pirates in Jamaica, outlaws treated like heroes and supported by the government and politicians, all while still being used by colonial powers.

But first, slavery would replace piracy as Jamaica's major source of income. By importing African slaves to Jamaica, the English had a free, disposable workforce to pick the sugarcane needed for rum and sugar to be sold in America and Europe.

The Spanish had owned slaves and after the Spanish were conquered by the British, instead of letting the new government enslave them, the free Maroons fled to the hills of Jamaica. The Maroons would fight against the British, led by Nanny, a female African leader who is now among Jamaica's national heroes. The Maroons would raid plantations, burn sugarcane fields, support African slaves in their revolts against their masters, and skirmish with British soldiers.

In 1731, the Maroons, made up of former Spanish slaves, native Jamaicans, and other slaves who'd escaped from the British, launched an all-out war against the English, using guerilla warfare tactics. Unable to defeat the Maroons, the British eventually wound up signing a treaty with them in 1739, giving them their own territory, but requiring them to return any runaway slaves and support the English in case of a Spanish or French invasion.

Another Maroon uprising in 1795 would lead to the deportation of several Maroons to Canada and Sierra Leone. The British would ban the importation of slaves in 1807 and slavery altogether in 1839, but the legacy of the slave revolts and the Maroon uprising still is very strong in Jamaican people. The rebel spirit to fight for independence and freedom is integral to the Jamaican spirit.

Like pirates, the Jamaican government run by the British co-opted the rebel Maroons. Both Henry Morgan and the rebel Maroon Nanny were outlaws allowed to live outside the realm of British law. Henry Morgan was a hero to the English, but an outlaw to others. Nanny was an undefeatable villain to the English. Rather than fighting her, they made a treaty with her, giving her people autonomy in return for protection against the Spanish.

The same reason Jamaica was an ideal place for pirates and important to the English and Spanish made it an ideal place for drug dealers and an important location for the U.S.. The drug-dealing Dons of the poor neighborhoods of Jamaica would be the new pirates: outlaws who protected and provided for their communities and were supported by the government. In a way they would also become the new Maroons, creating their own communities without any control from the government through unwritten deals with politicians.

Finally, in 1962 Jamaica gained independence from the British. While many Jamaicans, including Premier Norman Manley, wanted the country to unite with other Caribbean nations and join the Federation of the West Indies, Jamaica's first Prime Minister Alexander Bustamante (Manley's cousin) opposed the idea of being part of nation that combined all Caribbean countries. Despite the fact that Jamaica was independent, the country soon would learn that a new colonial power would be looking to control it, just like Spain and England had. This new colonial power was the United States of America.

Both Manley and Bustamante were activists in the fight for Jamaican voter and labor rights before independence. Bustamante, a charismatic leader, would form the Jamaican Labor Party (JLP) and Manley, a pragmatic lawyer, would form the People's National Party (PNP). Both men were light brown-skinned men of mixed heritage, who represented the mixed race upper class in Jamaica that would take over from the English ruling class.

Both political parties were tied to trade unions, which meant that supporters of the parties would have access to jobs if their parties were in power. In the beginning, there were not many political or philosophical differences between the two parties. Unlike the third-world countries in Africa, where the tribes would turn into political parties, in Jamaica the political parties would turn into tribes, fighting to ensure their own housing and jobs, which the government controlled.

The CIA could easily exploit all of these political, economic, and racial conflicts in Jamaica. By inflaming the tension between the JLP and the PNP, as well as driving the upper-class community against Michael Manley and his push for democratic socialism, the CIA would greatly harm the leadership of Michael Manley and bring a devastating cycle of drugs, guns, and heightened political warfare into the country.

Ironically, gangsters and drug dealers would replace the pirates who fought to protect Jamaica from outside forces. The British concept of the Robin Hood figure, which treated criminals as heroes and protectors of the poor, was used to turn pirates like Henry Morgan into legends. In order to preserve their empire, the British would employ these pirates for protection against the Spanish.

As British colonialism came to an end, it would be replaced by American neo-colonialism. Gold, spices, sugar, and slaves would be replaced by bauxite, guns, and drugs. Like the British, the U.S. would employ these new criminal heroes to help build their empire.

CHAPTER 2

THE DONS

One of Jamaica's dirtiest secrets is its connection between criminals and politicians. JLP leader Edward Seaga would establish the first politically based garrison in 1963 with Tivoli Gardens, which housed many of his supporters. The PNP would follow Seaga's lead, creating many garrison communities of their own, filled with poor and uneducated grassroots loyalists for their party. One of these garrison communities was Arnett Gardens, which would be built after Michael Manley and the PNP came into power in 1972. Both parties would use gang leaders to help get votes and consolidate their power. Politicians called these men community leaders, but in the communities they led, they were called other names.

These men were known as Dons, in homage to the Mafia kingpins popularized in American movies such as *The Godfather*. Like Don Corleone, these men were powerful leaders who would make money off gambling, prostitution, and illegal substances (marijuana). And just like the Godfather on his daughter's wedding day, they would give out favors to members of their community, earning their respect and loyalty. Some of these favors would include jobs and housing, which the Dons had access to due to their relationships with the politicians. In the film, when funeral director Amerigo Bonasera's daughter was brutally beaten, he came to the Godfather seeking justice after the legal system failed him. Similarly, members of these garrison communities came to their Dons for justice for beatings, rapes, burglaries, or murders and the Dons handed out justice for them with punishments of beatings and death.

The similarities between the community leaders and the Dons do not end there. In *The Godfather*, the gangster Barzini said "If Don Corleone had all the judges and the politicians in New York, then he must share them," and his cohort Tattaglia went as far as to say that he had the judges and politicians in his pocket.

Like Don Corleone, the Jamaican Dons had connections to politicians and judges that allowed them to operate without interference to the law, but it is unclear if the Dons had the politicians in their pocket or if the politicians had the Dons in theirs. The so-called community leaders did not need to bribe politicians for their support, but instead would provide the politicians with votes from their communities and manpower and weaponry for politically based clashes.

Gangsters helping politicians get votes is nothing new. In Chicago, Al Capone helped Chicago Mayor William Hale Thompson get elected by using his goons to throw grenades at polling places to disrupt voting. It has been alleged that John F. Kennedy's father, Joseph, used his old mob connection from his bootlegging days, getting notorious gangster Sam Giancana to help him get the votes in Chicago to win Illinois, which gave JFK the presidency.

The Italian Mafia in Sicily also wielded considerable power over the electorate and received immunity from the law from the politicians they helped elect. In 2013, the Minister of Justice in Japan was forced to resign due to alleged ties to the Yakuza.

In poor third-world countries, the international drug trade, fueled by Europe and America's hunger for cocaine and heroin, has only increased the ties between politicians and criminals to the point that they are now often one and the same. Notorious cocaine kingpin Pablo Escobar was elected to congress in 1982 in Colombia; former CIA agent and drug kingpin Manuel Noriega served as Prime Minister of Panama for six years before being deposed by the U.S..

Some of the Dons in Jamaica included Claudie Massop, who replaced Zackie the High Priest as the JLP Don of Tivoli Gardens after Zackie was killed. Massop served as Seaga's enforcer and liaison to Tivoli Gardens. Massop was respected and loved in his garrison as a tough yet benevolent authority figure and protector. An old lady who lived in Tivoli under Massop's rule told the *Jamaica Observer*:

> He was a nice person who anyone could approach, but he did not take kindly to rapists and petty thieves and dealt with them rough, and he was the one who set the real order and discipline in Tivoli Gardens. Claudie Massop was also our protector and he defended the community from attacks from our enemies in Matthews Lane and other PNP areas.

Massop was hated and feared by the people he viewed as enemies. A man who was a police officer in the time of Massop would tell the *Jamaica Observer* something completely different:

> That man was no saint. There are many who have felt his heavy hand and have suffered terrible human losses as a result. I was a constable at the time and was part of a patrol that came under heavy gunfire in the section of West Kingston where he reigned. In those days, rifles and submachine guns were just getting into the wrong hands and we did not have bulletproof vests or such big guns. We did not see who was actually firing at us; we got intelligence afterward that it was Massop

and his cronies. One of the cops in the patrol wet his pants.

The PNP was just as guilty when it came to associating with gangs and used Seaga's same tactic of providing housing and using gangsters for political support, both with bullets and ballots. One man who played a big part in that was Tony Spaulding. Tony Spaulding became Housing Minister after Michael Manley was elected in 1972 and began using that position to reward PNP supporters and displace JLP supporters.

Like Seaga, Spaulding had close ties with the communities he created and the gangsters who ran them. Spaulding helped build Arnett Gardens, a housing complex to rival Seaga's Tivoli Gardens. Spaulding's Arnett Gardens earned the name Concrete Jungle due to its vicious and tough atmosphere. Spaulding's man was Red Tony Welch, a ranking Don similar to Seaga's cohorts, Zackie the High Priest and Claudie Massop. Welch not only ran Arnett Gardens but he owned sound system Socialist Roots, the name being an homage to the PNP's new political position[1].

Another notorious enforcer was Winston "Burry Boy" Blake. Burry Boy would travel with Michael Manley everywhere as unofficial security. Rumor has it that Burry Boy saved Manley's life when he was shot at. Manley would pay tribute to Burry Boy by leading the funeral procession when Burry Boy was finally killed in a shoot-out[2].

The Dons would prove to be a potent weapon for the CIA. The CIA has a long and storied tradition of utilizing organized crime figures and politically based militias to further American

---

[1] Laurie Gunst, *Born Fi' Dead* (Macmillan, 1996) 92.

[2] Karyl Walker, Burry Boy and Feathermop: The violent duo that helped and shamed the PNP (The Jamaica Observer, 2008) http://www.jamaicaobserver.com/news/131579_Burry-Boy-and-Feathermop--The-violent-duo-that-helped-and-shamed-the-PNP

foreign policy. By bringing in the cocaine trade, the CIA would make the Dons more powerful than the politicians.

While Dons might have been kings of their respective garrison communities, they would be pawns in the Cold War. The JLP's Tivoli Garden leader Claudie Massop and the PNP's Bucky Marshall declared a truce and held a One Love Peace Concert headlined by Bob Marley. During that concert, Marley called opposing politicians Manley and Seaga to the stage in a sign of unity. Perhaps just as important, was reggae star Jacob Miller's performance, where he brought the top-ranking Dons, Earl "Tek Life" Wadley, Claudie Massop, and Aston "Bucky Marshall" Thompson and sang his song "Peace Treaty", which paid tribute to the truce between the ranking Jamaican gunmen.

But the truce would not last. The Dons who called the treaty would be killed and the war between PNP and JLP gunmen would escalate in 1980 during the bloodiest election in Jamaica up to that date. In suspicious circumstances, Jamaican police killed Claudie Massop, Marley's friend and driving force in the peace treaty. Massop would be replaced by Lester "Jim Brown" Coke, a warlord with no intent of bringing peace to Jamaica.

The Dons were not in control and did not have the power to make peace if the powers that be did not want peace. For the CIA and Seaga, a peaceful Jamaica under Manley would be a dangerous thing. If Manley could unite Jamaica and bring peace to the country, he would surely be re-elected and become a prominent leftist figure in the Caribbean. Seaga knew that his best chance of taking control of Jamaica was through violence, and the CIA knew that an unstable violent Jamaica would discredit Manley's democratic socialism and ruin his chance for reelection as well as dealing a blow to Cuba and leftist movements across the world.

The Dons would be the ghetto generals in the secret war between the PNP and the JLP. The CIA would support the JLP's ghetto generals and their militias through the arms and drug trade. This would lead to the ghetto generals being more powerful than the politicians they once served. The most famous Don of recent times, Christopher Dudus Coke—the son of Lester Jim Brown Coke, Edward Seaga's bodyguard and Don of Tivoli Gardens—would become so powerful that the Jamaican Prime Minister Bruce Golding would refuse to extradite him to the United States, eventually leading to the Prime Minister's resignation.

CHAPTER 3

ANGOLA

In late 1975, Henry Kissinger, the Secretary of State under then-American president Gerald Ford, paid a visit to Jamaica. Kissinger asked Manley to visit him at the Rockefeller estate in Ocho Rios and Manley refused, instead asking him to meet at Vale Royal, the official house of the Jamaican Prime Minister.

During their meeting Kissinger asked Manley to remain neutral and withdraw support for Fidel Castro's sending of troops to Angola. Castro had decided to send troops to Angola after the racist apartheid regime of South Africa invaded the country. Manley believed it was this refusal that led to the CIA campaign against him. Kissinger lied to Manley, telling him that the U.S. was impartial in the conflict, when in fact they were working with apartheid South Africa and white mercenaries at a high-scale level.

Kissinger had already met with President Ford, Defense Secretary James Schlesinger, and CIA Director William Colby to plan on aiding the South African-supported National Union for the Total Independence of Angola (UNITA) against the People's Movement for the Liberation of Angola (MPLA) led by Agostinho Neto. At Kissinger's request, President Ford eventually authorized covert CIA actions against the MPLA in support of UNITA. The presence of Cuban troops angered

Kissinger so much that he drew up plans to invade Cuba, but that never came into fruition[3].

John Stockwell used to coordinate CIA efforts in Angola. Stockwell was so disturbed by these actions in Angola that he became a whistleblower and revealed their dirty deeds to the world. Stockwell would talk about the CIA's operation in Jamaica in 1982:

> I observed that from published information the CIA station was quite large for a country of that size it was huge in fact bigger than any country I knew of in Africa, that's typical of when the CIA has got a big operation going on they beef up the station. Every indication of a massive CIA operation going to destabilize the government, to make the economy scream, in that case I would say someone got promoted several people. Without a scandal, without an assassination without the things that have caused the CIA so much grief, Manley a champion of social democracy, of giving the people a piece of the pie was thrown out of office and an arch-capitalist was put in office and there was minimal adverse publicity. Lou Wolf and me were studying the situation and I did publish about what was going on but it was not published in The New York Times or The Washington Post and the big TV stations. Primarily because even if they wanted to, due to the secrecy of what was going on they couldn't get the information on what the United States was really doing.

---

3 Frances Robles, Kissinger Drew Up Plans to Attack Cuba, Records Show (The New York Times, 2014) http://www.nytimes.com/2014/10/01/world/americas/kissinger-drew-up-plans-to-attack-cuba-records-show.html?_r=0

Stockwell knew very well the tactics the CIA was using in 1976, as he was their Station Chief in Angola, working under Bush during that year. Angola would be a key battleground in the war between the CIA and Castro. Manley's support of Castro's involvement came from his outrage against apartheid and the South African forces. The CIA had previously supported the apartheid regime in South Africa, by helping them capture a fugitive rebel leader by the name of Nelson Mandela.

Stockwell would later claim that CIA activities in Jamaica closely resembled the operation he conducted in Angola. Not only would he admit to carrying out illegal operations, but he would admit to lying about it to Congress. Of these experiences he would say:

> I testified for days before Congress, giving them chapter and verse, date and detail, proving specific lies. They were asking if we had to do with South Africa that was fighting in the country. In fact we were coordinating this operation so closely that our airplanes, full of arms from the States, would meet their airplanes in Kinshasa and they would take our arms into Angola to distribute to our forces for us....

> We had in fact formed four little mercenary armies and delivered them into Angola to do this dirty business for the CIA. And he lied to them about that. They asked if we were putting arms into the conflict, and he said no, and we were. They asked if we had advisors inside the country, and he said no, we had people going in to look at the situation and coming back out. In actuality we had 24 people sleeping inside the country, training in the use of weapons, installing communications systems, planning battles, and when testifying to Congress he said, we didn't have anybody inside the country.

In summary about Angola, without U.S. intervention, it's likely 10,000 people would have lived who were killed. The outcome might have been peaceful, or at least much less bloody. The MPLA was winning when we went in, and they went ahead and won, which was, according to our consul, the best thing for the country.

At the end of this thing the Cubans were entrenched in Angola, seen in the eyes of much of the world as heroes who saved these people from the CIA and South African forces. We had allied the U.S. literally and in the eyes of the world with the South African army, and that's illegal, and it's impolitic. We had hired white mercenaries and eventually been identified with them. And that's illegal, and it's impolitical. And our lies had been visible lies. We were caught out on those lies. And the world saw the U.S. as liars.[4]

Stockwell paints a clear picture of the CIA's tendency to conduct illegal operations abroad and then to lie about it to Congress and the media. Jamaica and Angola both were third-world countries caught in the crossfire of the Cold War, between American capitalism and Russian Communism.

Stockwell, like fellow CIA-agent-turned-whistleblower Philip Agee, would compare the CIA tactics in Jamaica to those in Chile, where a democratically elected president was replaced by a brutal dictator in 1973, and would come to the conclusion that there was a massive CIA operation being conducted in Jamaica. Stockwell would later talk about the CIA's secret wars: covert, low-intensity conflicts across the globe in the name of anti-Communism.

---

4 John Stockwell, America's Third World War, How 6 Million People Were Killed In CIA Secret Wars Against Third World Countries (Lecture, 1987) http://www.informationclearinghouse.info/article4068.htm

Stockwell would claim that his boss, George H.W. Bush, was more concerned with covering up illegal CIA activity than investigating it in Angola, and that Bush manipulated evidence of the CIA's role in the country. By showing vocal support for Castro in his war against CIA forces in Angola, Manley made himself and Jamaica targets in the CIA's secret war.

CHAPTER 4

MICHAEL MANLEY

Jamaica would first become a target for the CIA after it elected Michael Manley, the son of former premier and PNP founder Norman Manley. Michael was a World War II veteran, who combined his father's pragmatism with his cousin Bustamante's charisma and populist leading style. He graduated from the London School of Economics and worked in Jamaica as a journalist and as a negotiator for a trade union.

Manley was very inspired by the Civil Rights Movement and Black Power Movement in America. He used the slogan "giving power to the people" and initiated programs for the poor such as minimum wage, free education, rent control, healthcare, and land reform. Manley did not consider himself a Communist, and used the term Democratic Socialist to refer to his political beliefs.

It was not Manley's policies that angered the CIA but his friendship with and connection to Fidel Castro, the man who they unsuccessfully attempted to assassinate and overthrow. While Manley also had close ties to the leaders of countries friendly to the U.S. such as Sweden and Canada, he would quickly learn the old axiom *the friend of my enemy is my enemy* was a mantra that the CIA lived by.

It is understandable why the CIA, an organization that has always been dominated by the far-right in the U.S., would fear

Michael Manley. A Communist or even Democratic Socialist Jamaica could become a tipping point in the Caribbean. Jamaica was an English-speaking country that served as a vacation spot for the American elite. The Americans, like the Spanish and the British before them, realized Jamaica's ideal location for shipping and transport in the Caribbean and, like the Spanish and the British, were willing to fight for control of Jamaica at all costs.

Manley also had begun speaking out against the racist regimes in Angola and South Africa, two nations that the CIA was supporting. So, while not a Communist himself, Manley's progressive policies and refusal to distance himself from the CIA's public enemy number one, Fidel Castro, made him a target in the CIA and the U.S.'s Cold War on Communism. Manley with his ties to Castro and pro-Third World countries and anti-apartheid stance had placed himself smack-dab in the middle of that war.

Manley would welcome the Castro-backed MPLA from Angola, who were fighting against CIA and Apartheid South Africa-backed mercenaries. This would anger the American government, who requested that Jamaica not recognize the MPLA.

After meeting with Secretary of State Henry Kissinger regarding his support for Cuban troops in Angola, Manley would give a speech praising Cuba's action in Angola, saying that Castro saved "Jamaica's black brothers and sisters" in Angola from conquest by racist apartheid South African imperialism[5].

---

5 Ellen Ray, CIA And Local Gunmen Plan Jamaican Coup (Counterspy Magazine, 1976) http://jfk.hood.edu/Collection/Weisberg%20Subject%20Index%20Files/C%20Disk/Committee%20For%20Action%20and%20Research%20on%20the%20Inteligence%20Community/Item%2011.pdf

In the 70s, as colonialism was coming to an end, Manley would identify with the Non-Aligned Movement, which included several Asian, African, and other Third World countries. These included developing countries that chose not to ally themselves with either Communist Russia or capitalist America. The Non-Aligned Movement would protest against colonialism, neo-colonialism, and racism.

This alone was enough to anger the United States and the CIA, which caused CIA patron, George H.W. Bush's son to say, "You are either with us, or you are against us." The CIA's course of actions prove they'd prefer a right-wing dictator run a country than a socially progressive democratically elected leader.

Manley would undertake massive education, labor, health, and housing reform. Many of these reforms would benefit the poor and uneducated lower class of Jamaica. These reforms would scare the American right wing and the CIA into believing he could become a Jamaican Castro.

Ambassador Gerard would paint a clear picture of the U.S. government's views on Manley in a cable sent in January of 1976:

> There are definitely changes in traditional attitudes towards the U.S. insofar as the GOJ is concerned. PM Manley's love affair with Castro, his aspirations for Third World leadership, and his own ideological inclinations seem to assure a continuing drift in foreign policy to the left, and thus an increasing range of friction points in our bilateral relationships. On the other hand, despite efforts to diversify Jamaica's bauxite alumina market, Jamaica will remain dependent on the U.S. market for some years to come. This, together with the importance of the tourist industry and geographic proximity, would seem

to assure that whatever may happen in the foreign affairs realm there will be close economic ties for the foreseeable future.

Manley's support of Cuban troops in Angola and anger at the oppressive Apartheid South African regime was also a point of contention for Gerard:

> Manley and many other key Jamaican leaders are emotional to the point of irrationality on the subject of South Africa. South Africa's intervention in Angola, coupled with Manley's love affair with Cuba, thus assured sympathy for Cuba's involvement.[6]

The CIA has a long history of trying to undermine progressive leaders. They helped the South African government find and arrest Nelson Mandela, tried to assassinate Patrice Lumumba, and overthrew progressive Chilean leader Salvador Allende, replacing him with right wing narco-dictator, Augusto Pinochet.

Manley posed a big threat for the CIA, which acted in the interest of neo-colonialism and imperialism. Both his foreign and domestic policy represented the opposite of what the CIA wanted for Third World countries. His association with the CIA's arch nemesis and Jamaica's closest neighbor Cuba did not help. Manley was compared to both Kennedy and Castro; his charisma, good looks, and oratory skills would make him a dangerous representative for both Jamaica and the Third World.

Manley's nemesis, Edward Seaga, was a viable alternative to the CIA. Seaga wasn't racist or classist; he was very generous and supportive to the poor black people who lived in Tivoli Gardens. However, Seaga told American officials that he would

---

6 US Embassy In Jamaica Cable (JAMAICAN PERCEPTIONS OF THE U.S.) https://www.wikileaks.org/plusd/cables/1976KINGST00310_b.html

not interfere in global politics and would welcome American business. He also had a long history of anti-Cuban and anti-Communist rhetoric that fell in line with the CIA's thinking. Unlike Manley, who seemed to be motivated by ideology and the desire for change, Seaga seemed to be motivated by power. The CIA used this motivation, along with the loyalty of his gunmen, to fight Manley.

CHAPTER 5

JAMAICA AND THE USA

The relationship between Manley and the U.S. was never a strong one. In 1973, the U.S. Ambassador to Jamaica Vincent De Roulet was a multi-millionaire who had received his ambassadorship under Nixon. De Roulet came to Jamaica with a 90-foot yacht and a fleet of racehorses. He would belittle the Jamaican people by calling them idiots, children, and reportedly niggers. De Roulet was known to be a racist who said that Jamaican Prime Minister Hugh Shearer was an "anti-Communist, courteous, and well dressed Negro who didn't talk about his little people with their withering bellies and the back to Africa crap and knew where his bread was buttered."[7]

According to Frederick Irving, who was the U.S. Ambassador to Jamaica in 1977, when Manley first tried to shake De Roulet's hand, the ambassador replied, "Sorry Mr. Prime Minister, but I don't shake hands with a black man."

The Nixon-appointed ambassador saw Jamaica as "the dregs of foreign service," and believed it was the role of the Americans to civilize the foreign savages. He said that Jamaicans were the most spoiled race in the world, saw Manley as a socialist threat to U.S. interests, and viewed Manley as a "racially confused, latent alcoholic."

---

7 Randolph B. Persaud, *Counter-Hegemony and Foreign Policy* (SUNY Press, 2001) 160.

De Roulet disliked Manley for other reasons. Jamaica has a great deal of bauxite, the material needed to make aluminum. Four of the five bauxite companies that operate in Jamaica are American-owned; the other is Canadian-owned. There had been talk about nationalizing the bauxite industry, which would have hurt the American aluminum companies. Manley's economic aides had encouraged him to make bauxite nationalization a campaign issue in the 1972 election against Hugh Shearer. This angered De Roulet, who had organized payments from the aluminum company Alcoa to the JLP.

Despite the fact that De Roulet looked down on Manley and was a supporter of the JLP's Hugh Shearer, he hedged his bets and attempted to make a deal with Michael Manley to protect U.S. bauxite interests. De Roulet testified before Congress that he made a deal with Michael Manley before the election in 1972, that America would not interfere with the election if Manley did not make nationalization of the mostly foreign-owned bauxite companies a campaign issue. Others construe these words as a threat; De Roulet was warning Manley would lose the election with CIA interference if he made bauxite nationalization an issue.

Manley denied that he made the deal and responded by kicking De Roulet out of Jamaica and declaring the ambassador persona non grata. He may have denied this partly from fear of seeming weak in the face of U.S. pressure. De Roulet was later involved in the Watergate scandal when it was charged that he gave Nixon's campaign a $100,000 donation. It is believed this contribution and others by his family got his ambassadorship transferred to Europe.

De Roulet was a personification of much that was wrong with America: rich, arrogant, racist, and determined to meddle in Jamaican affairs and elections in the interest of American companies. His replacement was another rich Republican, Sumner Gerard who, unlike De Roulet, seemed to have some knowledge and tact when it came to diplomacy. Still, like De Roulet, Gerard was pro-JLP.

Frederick Irving, the ambassador who replaced Gerard, claimed that Gerard was "almost as bad [as De Roulet] and interfered openly and blatantly in local elections in Jamaica." Irving also spoke of De Roulet and Gerard's relationship with Seaga and the JLP: "Apparently, our two ambassadors had a close relationship with Seaga and it was a question in my mind as to who is running the embassy, Seaga or our ambassadors."

Irving had a quite different relationship with Seaga. When Irving told Seaga that he'd remain neutral in PNP and JLP affairs, Seaga angrily said, "Then you're going to have a hard time here, and I'm going to see to it."[8]

Gerard was very aware of the political situation in Jamaica and the connections of the politicians to armed criminals. While cynical about Seaga, he clearly saw the JLP as a better option for American interests and wrote about Seaga's need for guns in a recently declassified 1976 cable:

> Lest anyone be in doubt, Seaga is no angel, but if anything he is rational. As an opposition leader he gets only one shot, and that the embassy believes he will save for the general election. Power is his goal and that can only be achieved through the ballot-box. He needs his gunmen to assure safe passage for his supporters to the polling station.

---

8 Frederick Irving, Interview, Jamaica - Association for Diplomatic Studies and Training http://adst.org/wp-content/uploads/2012/09/Jamaica1.pdf

While Gerard acknowledged Seaga's need for gunmen to put him in power, he actively tried to stop the PNP from using gunmen of their own. He sent a letter to airport and law enforcement agencies about an Eric Rico Walton who was said to be importing weapons from Chicago.

On the eve of the election, both the U.S. Government and Seaga realized that violence was a possibility. Seaga even envisioned the election resulting in guerilla warfare, which he was looking forward to, according to Gerard.

> It is a strong possibility the radical fringe of the PNP might not accept the election results and could resort to violence perhaps urban guerrilla warfare in Kingston. He (Seaga) rather hoped this would happen. It would give him an opportunity to clean up that problem once and for all. The security forces were completely sympathetic with him and would like nothing better than to be turned loose against the violent left of Jamaican politics. It would take no more than a month.[9]

The American Embassy also saw guerilla warfare as a possibility, and envisioned a scenario where Cuban forces would be called on to keep the peace. Brigadier Jerry Green, the head of the Jamaican Defense Force, was an informant for the American government, providing the embassy with information. Green told the embassy that Manley was planning a state of emergency in January after the IMF meeting was disrupted by bombing and riots, but that Green had persuaded Manley against taking such action. Green also relayed to the U.S. government that the PNP

---

9 US Embassy In Jamaica Cable (Opposition Leader Seaga Confident He Will Be Jamaica's Next Prime Minister) https://wikileaks.org/plusd/cables/1976Kingsto4896_b.html

government had discussions about arresting Seaga, but decided not to, in fear of creating a political martyr. The embassy also had information from Colonel Leslie Lloyd Defense Intelligence Agency agent in Venezuela and number-two man at the JDF that Manley had planned on calling in not the British or the Americans, but the Cubans.

Gerard and the U.S. Government kept track of PNP construction workers being trained in Cuba as well as Cubans providing logistical assistance in Jamaica. Cables show that Gerard was afraid of several scenarios that would lead to Cuban intervention in the election and the possible presence of Cuban troops.

Manley and Gerard both withheld information from each other. Manley was probably afraid that Gerard was sharing information. The ambassador was also angered when ex-CIA agent Philip Agee came to Jamaica and named several CIA agents in the American Embassy. Gerard was afraid that Manley would call out the U.S. over the CIA agents Agee named and ban them from the country. Gerard was convinced that Manley was behind the Agee affair and wanted to be recalled for consultations, in diplomatic protest and to have U.S. aid to Jamaica reduced.

It's not clear if the ambassador was working with the CIA or even was aware of their activities. He had a very cynical attitude to Manley's destabilization charges. Gerard was keeping a close eye on activities of Manley's Housing Minister Anthony Spaulding, DK Duncan, PNP Youth Leader Luis Castriota, and left-wing professor Trevor Munroe and their statements about the CIA.

A lot of Gerard's job in 1976 was to deny CIA activity in Jamaica. After the IMF riots in Jamaica in January, Gerard met with American and Jamaican businessmen to dispel rumors of CIA or American involvement in Jamaican politics. He would state that the accusations of CIA involvement came from organizations involved with the Jamaican government.

Dudley Thompson, Michael Manley's Minister of Foreign affairs, would meet with Gerard in April about American foreign policy and possible CIA involvement in Jamaica. Thompson would refer to a story in the *New York Daily News* with the headline "Is The U.S. Setting The Scene For Intervention In Jamaica" in meeting with Jamaican diplomats. Thompson would tell Gerard historically, the U.S. has intervened where it could save a particular country from Communism.

Thompson would criticize the U.S. about its policy in Angola and praise the Cubans for intervening against forces supported by apartheid South Africa. He would also criticize U.S. support of military dictatorships in Latin America.

Thompson also brought up an article in *The New York Times* by James Reston that quoted senior officials saying the Jamaican police were being trained in Cuba. Reston was a close friend of Henry Kissinger, and was later revealed to be a press agent for the CIA who they used to promote their views. Reston was part of an initiative by the CIA called Operation Mockingbird that used hundreds of journalists for CIA propaganda.

In a cable from May of 1976, the U.S. Embassy would attempt to predict the role of the United States in that year's election, making it clear that he saw the PNP as an enemy of the U.S. and the JLP as a friend.

> Both parties will attempt to involve the U.S. in the election campaign. The PNP will use the U.S. as a scapegoat, to divert public attention from its own domestic failures. Accusations of destabilization efforts already are being heard. The JLP will quietly

solicit our support and funds to stop what it considers Jamaica's march to Communism under Manley.[10]

Gerard would steadfastly and consistently deny CIA involvement in Jamaica, despite the CIA office that was on the third floor of the embassy he worked in. Gerard may not have been lying, but he wasn't telling the truth.

The CIA and the U.S. Government have a tactic called plausible deniability, which involves the CIA withholding information from senior officials. That way, the official is able to deny any illegal or unscrupulous activities by the CIA and shift blame without being held responsible. Still, Gerard was very concerned with allegations against the CIA and was particularly concerned with the safety of the CIA agents who were named by Agee.

While the agents in the embassy that Gerard worked with must have been known to him, it's not clear if he knew exactly what they were doing. Still, he was clearly being given information from the JLP and had a healthy distrust and animosity toward the PNP and their officials.

---

10 US Embassy In Jamaica Cable (JAMAICA - POLITICAL TRENDS ANALYSIS) https://wikileaks.org/plusd/cables/1976KINGST02075_b.html

CHAPTER 6

STATE OF EMERGENCY

In 1976, Manley and the PNP began insinuating that the CIA had an active destabilization plan for Jamaica. Like ex-CIA agents Philip Agee and John Stockwell, PNP leaders would compare the CIA's role in Jamaica to its role in Chile: overthrowing elected leader Salvador Allende followed by a military coup. One of those most fiercely suspicious of the CIA was PNP Foreign Minister Dudley Thompson, who would say:

> The object of a campaign mounted from the United States similar to the one which preceded the overthrow of President Salvador Allende in Chile in 1973.

Michael Manley would say:

> I cannot prove in a court of law that the CIA is here. What I have said are strange things are happening in Jamaica that we have not seen before.

Manley would also allege that the violence in Jamaica was being caused by what he called destabilization agents and give a description of destabilization that was a veiled reference to the CIA.

Let me tell you how destabilization works, they will go in, this secret group that is trying to mash up the country, they will go in among the youth and find one that looks like a leader, and they call him on side and say hey brother, we'll drop you $1000 on the side if you get the boys tomorrow night to go down across the road and carry out a raid but they don t know it is a destabilization agent, that has paid somebody to come among them and sell the idea to start a bitch of a street fight.[11]

There were several events leading up to the state of emergency beginning in 1976. In January during the IMF conference, leftist groups protested the apartheid South African delegate. The protest then marched to the American consulate, where Ambassador Sumner Gerard called for Jamaican police protection. The two policemen who came to guard the Consulate were murdered. Counterspy Magazine's Ellen Ray would claim that these murders were the start of a CIA organized plan of terror in Jamaica. Other bombings and acts of violence would coincide with these murders, giving visiting journalists an impression of Jamaica as a violent and unstable country.

In May 1976, a housing complex in the PNP area of Trenchtown was felled by an arson attack when armed men blocked off the exits and threw Molotov cocktails into the area. People fleeing the area were shot at and eight children were killed in the incident while 500 would be left homeless. Both the PNP and the JLP would blame each other for the violence.

Ellen Ray wrote an article for Counterspy called, "CIA and Local Gunmen Plan Jamaican Coup." In the article, she wrote that 20 gunmen attacked a PNP youth dance in 1976 with

---

11   *Blood And Fire* (Documentary) https://www.youtube.com/watch?v=ZO5lTRMg-Js

machine guns, killing six and wounding 50. Ray claimed the gunmen killed a wounded woman by shooting at the ambulance that was taking her to the hospital.

The Counterspy article also noted bombings, gun shipments, poisoning of flower shipments, and burning cane fields for agricultural sabotage as incidents that fell in line with the CIA's terror campaign in Jamaica[12].

A former JLP organizer, Herb Rose, would defect from the party in early June of 1976. He claimed that the JLP's political strategy was based on violence, arson, and murder; and that he had seen top JLP leaders giving out guns to youngsters and training them in violence[13].

Also in June, the Peruvian Ambassador to Jamaica, Fernando Rodríguez Oliva would be stabbed to death in his own home. The crime would go unsolved, but would fit a pattern of CIA-sponsored anti-Cuban terrorism that would target embassies, ambassadors, and government officials all over Latin America and the Caribbean in 1976.

Accusing the CIA is easy; catching them in the act is very hard. In 1976, Jamaican officials in the PNP attempted to have their own spies provide information on the CIA and the JLP. One informer who earned the name Albert "Spy" Robinson was instructed to infiltrate the CIA and the JLP; to trade tapes of PNP meetings and pamphlets for a visa. Robinson was directed to one of Seaga's aides, whom he met in Ocho Rios. When he could not get to Seaga, he was told to go to James Holt, a CIA officer posing as Head of Security at the American Embassy.

---

12 Ellen Ray, *CIA And Local Gunmen Plan Jamaican Coup* (Counterspy Magazine, 1976) http://jfk.hood.edu/Collection/Weisberg%20Subject%20Index%20Files/C%20Disk/Committee%20For%20Action%20and%20Research%20on%20the%20Inteligence%20Community/Item%2011.pdf

13 Kareen Felicia Williams, *The Evolution of Political Violence in Jamaica 1940-1980* (Columbia University, 2011) 216.

Holt would later be accused of using Robinson's tapes as part of a plan to turn the Jamaican military against the Manley government.

Robinson then brought information he obtained from his JLP infiltration and gave it to Assistant Police Commissioner C.S. Griffiths, and it was shared with Michael Manley, D.K. Duncan, and other PNP officials. Robinson would also bring a gun to Seaga's underlings and claim that PNP minister D.K. Duncan gave it to him.

The information obtained by Robinson led to the PNP claiming they had uncovered a JLP/CIA plot to violently overthrow the government. Jamaican security services would arrest several JLP members, including Peter Whittingham, a former member of the Jamaican Defense Force (JDF) and Pearnel Charles, who the American ambassador referred to as a "JLP thug." Charles would be charged with Conspiracy to Commit Murder with "persons unknown" and be acquitted the next year when the prosecution's witness recanted their statement.

Manley claimed that the police discovered documents in Whittingham's briefcase called Operation Werewolf, which outlined a plot to overthrow the government. In these documents were references to 23 trained men, 200 rifles, 100 submachine guns, two barrels of gunpowder, and 50,000 anti-government pamphlets. Manley also said that the language and intention of these documents were subversive, violent and are concerned with terrorism and even the overthrow of the government of Jamaica[14].

Along with the documents found, police would also find five revolvers, two loaded submachine guns, and 431 rounds

---

14 US Embassy In Jamaica Cable (MEETING WITH PRIME MINISTER MANLEY) https://search.wikileaks.org/plusd/cables/1976KINGST03115_b. html

of ammunition[15]. This alleged plot to overthrow the government and the recent violence would cause Manley to declare a state of emergency in Jamaica on June 22, 1976. He immediately began locking up hundreds of JLP supporters he believed were involved in the alleged conspiracy. Manley claimed that Peter Whittingham's documents urged the people to take up arms against the Prime Minister and was similar to the CIA -supported coup in Chile.

The Jamaican ambassador to the U.S. went to the State Department and warned of a plot of Miami-based Jamaican exiles against the government of Jamaica. Manley would also claim the Royal Mounted Canadian Police assisted him in learning about the plot, which also involved Jamaican exiles in Toronto[16]. Much of the information on these plots came from C.S. Griffiths, the man who had set up Robinson as a spy.

Manley would make a speech justifying the state of emergency, hinting at a conspiracy against Jamaica:

> In the course of investigating this strange and sinister case, other and similar matters came to light suggesting at the very least the possibility of a conspiracy to create harm to the name of prominent supporters of the government.

Three days after Manley declared the state of emergency, CIA Director Bush met with President Ford and said he was

---

15 Lowell Sutherland, *Nine Arrested Under Manley's New Powers* (Associated Press, 1976) https://news.google.com/newspapers?nid=757&dat=19760 623&id=7nVaAAAAIBAJ&sjid=AEcDAAAAIBAJ&pg=4288,2877964&hl=en

16 *Police Infiltrate Plotters* (The Virgin Island Daily News, 1976) https://news.google.com/newspapers?nid=757&dat=19760716&id=_2ZSAAAAIBAJ &sjid=9EYDAAAAIBAJ&pg=4844,1761582&hl=en

concerned about the charges being made against the CIA in Jamaica according to his notes.

Ten days after the state of emergency, American ambassador Sumner Gerard sent a cable titled *State of Emergency: Albert Robinson*. According to the cable, Seaga believed the state of emergency was called because Manley feared that the JLP would go public with the information they'd received from the PNP's spy. The cable showed that the embassy was scared of what Manley's spy might know or say.

> Robinson was a PNP organizer and youth leader, which might explain Manley's reaction. The P.M. may have had reason to believe Robinson did have some embarrassing information to peddle. The embassy would be tempted to dismiss the whole episode as a sad farce if it were not for the fact that Robinson in his bumbling way has succeeded in creating a situation in which the prestige and credulity of the P.M., the opposition leader and the Brigadier are very much at stake.[17]

The opposition leader was Edward Seaga, and the brigadier was Rudolph Green, who had previously provided the embassy/CIA with information on Michael Manley. It seems as if the police force and C.S. Griffiths were allied with Manley and the PNP, while the army and JDF was allied with Seaga, the JLP, and the CIA.

Manley would later meet with U.S. Ambassador Sumner Gerard and discuss the state of emergency and Alvin Robinson. Gerard would assure Manley that there were no covert actions

---

17 US Embassy In Jamaica Cable (STATE OF EMERGENCY: ALBERT ROBINSON) https://www.wikileaks.org/plusd/cables/1976KINGST02739_b.html

by the CIA in Jamaica and when the issue of Albert "Spy" Robinson came up, Manley did not disclose that Robinson was in fact a spy, charged with infiltrating the CIA and the JLP, and instead dismissing him as a psychopath. Gerard was suspicious of Manley's story and would write in a U.S. cable:

> There was an Alice In Wonderland quality to the conversation. Robinson, the psychopath, told the opposition that he had received an unlicensed weapon from PNP Sec. Gen. D K Duncan.

> No, the PM assures me, that is not true, the gun was licensed and given to him by the police commissioner. I was tempted to ask, but did not, when the police commissioner had started distributing revolvers to psychopaths.

> Given Manley's predisposition to believe we are behind all of his troubles and the keystone cop performance of his security forces when it comes to handling and evaluating intelligence, I believe we must be very careful and selective in passing information to the Government of Jamaica (GOJ), lest we unnecessarily inflame an already nervous and paranoiac group.[18]

The interaction between Gerard and Manley is very telling. Manley was in no position to tell Gerard that Robinson was in fact a spy. Gerard, it seemed, was dedicated to covering up the work of the CIA in 1976.

Sumner Gerard had all the markings of a CIA officer himself. He was a World War II veteran who became a Captain of Intelligence for the Navy, and went on to be the Director

---

18 US Embassy In Jamaica Cable (MEETING WITH PRIME MINISTER MANLEY) https://search.wikileaks.org/plusd/cables/1976KINGST03115_b.html

for USAID in Tunisia. USAID is well known as a CIA front company in the third world. Cables sent from Gerard indicate a strong hatred of Manley and the PNP and many refer to allegations of CIA activities in Jamaica.

Manley's call for the state of emergency seems to have been justified. He seemed genuinely fearful of plots against them and had more than enough reason to believe the CIA was partially behind them. What information Robinson got from CIA agent James Holt may never be revealed; Holt was transferred from Jamaica in September of that year after being unmasked as a CIA agent by another former agent.

Both Manley and Gerard were lying to each other. Gerard also asked Manley about a recent bomb that went off at the Norman Manley International Airport, named after Michael's father. Manley believed Cuban exiles were behind the attack. Gerard knew exactly who did the bombing: two CIA agents who were still working very closely with the agency.

On July 17, 1976, the Jamaican Ambassador to the United States gave information to the United States government about a plot to cause mass disruption and violence during a Caribbean festival, which was slated to be on July 23rd.

According to the information, a confidential Jamaican informant living in Miami was approached by a Cuban exile and recruited to join a group of Jamaicans to overthrow the government of Jamaica due its close ties to Cuba and Communism.

The informant claims he was later approached by another Jamaican, Everton Pearte, who recruited him to join a group of Jamaicans traveling to Jamaica from the U.S., to commit acts of terrorism through bombing and burning during the Caribbean Festival, Carifesta.

According to the informant, the explosives would be shipped to Jamaica from the U.S. and 40 Jamaican expatriates would target Jamaican public utilities and water supplies as well as businesses and poor people's houses.

After the informant managed to discourage Pearte from participating in the attacks, he claimed that Pearte was murdered by people who wanted to make sure that he did not compromise the operation. According to the informant, the operation was financed by Cuban exiles and that the Jamaican terrorists were also involved in the drug trade[19].

While the information did not determine the identities of the Cuban exiles who were funding and organizing the Jamaicans to engage in terrorism, previous information furnished from Michael Manley had their informant giving information leading to the terrorist organization Alpha 66. Alpha 66 was an anti-Cuban terrorist organization under the umbrella of Orlando Bosch's CORU.

The connection between the CIA and the Cuban exiles in Miami is very strong and it is clear that Jamaica was targeted by these Cuban exiles. These Cubans were also big players in the cocaine trade. Given that they were allies against the Manley government in Jamaica, it is a safe assumption to make that the guns, drugs and terrorism were coming in with assistance from the anti-Castro Cubans and by extension, the CIA.

In October of 1978, the issue of CIA interference in Jamaica returned during a corruption trial for Michael Manley, in which Albert "Spy" Robinson testified. Police commissioner C.S. Griffiths would testify and play recordings he had of Robinson. According to the tapes, Robinson told Griffiths that he was

---

19 US Embassy In Jamaica Cable (ALLEGED TERRORIST ACTIVI-TIES PLANNED FOR JAMAICA) https://search.wikileaks.org/plusd/cables/1976STATE179022_b.html

aware of a CIA plot to kill Fidel Castro in Jamaica. Griffiths would testify that Robinson was used by Manley and the PNP to spy on the JLP and he discovered links between Edward Seaga and several CIA agents including James Holt, who was working undercover at the U.S. Embassy under the title of Regional Security Officer.

Griffiths would claim that Holt offered Robinson a U.S. visa and protection in return for information on the PNP. According to Griffiths, Robinson, at the request of and help of Holt, would travel to Toronto for training by the CIA. According to cables from the U.S. Embassy, during the trial it was alleged that Holt was a CIA agent who offered Robinson employment, loaned him $200, and attempted to recruit Robinson to assassinate Fidel Castro. The cables also showed that Robinson met with Holt at least five times at the U.S. Embassy.

Robinson would tell Holt that he had traveled to Cuba on several occasions for military training and knew of a Cuban plot to take over Jamaica by force if the JLP won the 1976 election. According to Holt, Robinson would bring him tapes recorded in Cuba as well as pamphlets from Havana and Moscow. Robinson would also travel to Toronto, Canada and meet with a U.S. official who would give him a visa to travel to the United States, where he would meet with a reporter from The New York Times[20].

During the trial, Robinson would claim that he was being threatened and intimidated by unknown forces, who would throw Molotov cocktails at his house and force his family to flee. Robinson would claim to have tapes that proved he was a spy for Michael Manley but would never produce them. He

---

20 US Embassy In Jamaica Cable ("SPY" ROBINSON AND AL-LEGATIONS AGAINST HOLT) https://search.wikileaks.org/plusd/cables/1978KINGST08634_d.html

would contradict many of his statements made on tape during Manley's corruption trial alleging CIA and JLP involvement in plots against the Manley government during his testimony.

Still, the evidence is clear that Robinson met several times with Holt and that Holt was a CIA agent. Manley would claim to Ambassador Irving in 1978 that Robinson was under a truth serum when he made his allegations against the CIA in 1976. Embassy cables show that Holt and Robert Houdek (another embassy official named as a CIA agent) were involved in some sort of plot involving Canadian officials and Robinson.

Given the embassy cables that have recently been released by Wikileaks, it is quite obvious that Robinson was indeed a spy for Manley who managed to infiltrate the CIA and the JLP. Given that he had a criminal record, there is no way he could have traveled to Canada and the United States without help from the U.S. Embassy. The New York Times reporter that Robinson met with was most likely James Reston, who would write a story with information similar to the information that Robinson would tell Holt about Cubans training Jamaican forces. Reston was a reporter closely affiliated with the CIA.

James Holt and Robert Houdek were both named by Philip Agee as CIA agents and given the fact that both of them went on to careers in the intelligence field, it is clear that both men were CIA agents during their stay in Jamaica. Michael Manley seems to have managed to outspy the CIA with his use of Robinson, who was a double agent, which led to him calling the state of emergency and his strong belief of an active campaign by the CIA to destabilize his government. Embassy cables also show that Manley held back on bringing up his proof of CIA destabilization in Jamaica in the hopes of maintaining a good relationship with the United States.

CHAPTER 7

SEAGA

In the CIA's eyes, the JLP's Edward Seaga was an ideal candidate to replace Manley. Seaga was born in Boston to Jamaican parents of Syrian, Indian, Lebanese, and Scottish heritage. He went to Jamaica as a baby, later attending the prestigious Wolmer's School and returning to Boston to attend Harvard University.

Seaga was very similar to Manley: a brown-skinned man of the Jamaican upper class who related to and received the adulation of the Jamaican poor and working classes. Seaga built his base with the poor people of Kingston as a music promoter and producer. He was nominated to Parliament by Alexander Bustamante and was later elected to Parliament for the West Kingston district in the 60s.

One of Seaga's first acts was the building of the Tivoli Gardens housing community in Kingston, in a slum known as Back-O-Wall. In doing so, Seaga displaced many of the Rastafarian residents and PNP supporters and the Tivoli housing development would be used to house his JLP supporters.

Seaga became a hero in Tivoli Gardens. He would take the young people to the movies and buy residents chicken and ice cream while stressing the importance of education. To this day, Seaga is seen as a patron and protector of Tivoli Gardens; there remains a soccer stadium named after him.

Seaga was not as kind to neighborhoods not allied to the JLP. In 1965, during a speech at the 100th anniversary of the Morant Bay slave rebellion, Seaga was heckled. "If they think they are bad," he shouted, "I can bring the crowds of West Kingston. We can deal with you in any way at any time. It will be fire for fire, and blood for blood."[21]

The crowds of West Kingston, aka the Phoenix Gang, were led by Zackie the High Priest. Seaga had close ties to Zackie, known to be one of the first ranking dons of Jamaica. Seaga clashed with PNP Senator Dudley Thompson, who had the support of his own PNP gangs, mainly The Spanglers and The Vikings. The two would spar over land and housing for their respective supporters. Under the direction of Seaga, bulldozers destroyed makeshift residences of PNP supporters to build houses for JLP loyalists. The leader of The Vikings was called Dillinger, named after the notorious American bank robber immortalized in Hollywood movies.

Seaga proved true to his word, and the Phoenix Gang began an extremely violent clash with the PNP-affiliated gangs, The Vikings and The Spanglers. The attacks included, on both sides, use of guns and makeshift bombs such as dynamite and Molotov cocktails.

Dillinger wound up killing Zackie the High Priest and the violence escalated, with gangs on both sides fighting one another and the police until a state of emergency was called. Seaga would blame the PNP, claiming they had started something merciless and cruel, the end result is unknown, and may well provoke massive retaliation and death. Norman Manley (Michael's father) would blame Seaga, saying, "Seaga's private army is well armed and the new element was introduced when

---

21 Laurie Gunst, *Born Fi Dead* (New York: Macmillan, 1996) 84.

he made his threat last year of blood for blood and fire for fire and threatened to use that private army."[22]

As early as 1966, Seaga was accusing the PNP of bringing in guns from Cuba, claiming that PNP politicians brought in weapons to increase their power. During the months between the state of emergency and the 1967 elections, police would raid both PNP and JLP headquarters in West Kingston, finding guns, ammunition, and Molotov cocktails. Though the violence would subside after the election, Thompson and Seaga would start a vicious cycle of politicians and gang leaders fighting to control territory and the country as a whole.

Michael Manley's bodyguard and PNP Don Burry Boy had faced murder charges. Tony Spaulding, the lawyer who would become PNP Housing Minister, would successfully defend him against those charges, and many politicians would also serve as lawyers for the gunmen that served their party. Burry Boy was said to travel with a gang of thirty men on Honda motorcycles, terrorizing JLP territory and headquarters. Much like their Mafia counterparts, the politically connected Jamaican gangsters would become early Teflon Dons: no charges would ever stick.

Burry Boy played a dual role as Manley's secret service agent and the PNP's enforcer in the ghettos. He was rewarded for his loyalty with lucrative government contracts and he traveled to Cuba with his patron Manley.

When Burry Boy was shot and killed, more than 20,000 people came to his funeral, many of them the poor people who saw him as a protector and hero for their communities. Michael Manley, along with several other PNP cabinet members, led Burry Boy's funeral procession. While Burry Boy was a hero to the masses, to many others, such as the Tivoli residents, he was

---

22 Terry Lacey, Violence and Politics in Jamaica, 1960-70: (Manchester University Press, 1977) 89.

a villain. When the funeral procession passed, Tivoli residents took it as a sign of disrespect and shot at the PNP supporters mourning their fallen hero.

When Manley resigned as prime minister in 1992, he said his biggest mistake in judgment was attending the funeral of Burry Boy, which he said sent the wrong message: that he supported gangsters, political violence, and the glorification of the gunman. The truth was, both the PNP and JLP glorified and co-opted the outlaw hero paradigm. The English had turned to pirate Henry Morgan for protection against the Spanish and French and in return, they gave him money, power and glory, so had the PNP and JLP co-opted the Don.

While technically, there was no civil war in Jamaica, the tensions between the PNP and the JLP both in politics and street warfare were easily exploited by the CIA. The connections between ballots and bullets meant that the CIA could easily assist the JLP with the tactics used in many civil wars.

When asked about his connection with the CIA, Seaga later said, "We did not receive any help from the CIA. In any event, a good CIA operative does not declare his presence."[23] This seemed to indicate that in fact Seaga did receive help from the CIA but he was discreet, giving himself plausible deniability.

---

23 Dwight Bellafante, Pearnel still seeking compensation for 1976 detention (The Jamaica Observer, 2006) http://www.jamaicaobserver.com/news/107411_Pearnel-still-seeking-compensation-for-1976-detention

CHAPTER 8

JAMAICA COCAINE HUB

As in the case of Nicaragua and Laos, there is also evidence that the CIA used a similar strategy in Jamaica of using the drug trade to empower the right-wing political party supported by the U.S.

In Laos, the CIA facilitated General Vang Pao's heroin-dealing operation through their airline Air America, so he could have the money and the power to fight the Communist forces in his country.[24] In Nicaragua, the CIA would help many people involved with the Contras with cocaine trafficking.[25]

The drug trade is an ideal way to support armed Third World forces. America can arm and support these groups and the drug trade gives them a source of income that is very hard to trace back to the U.S. The global illegal weapons and drug trade often go hand-in-hand and involve the same players, providing an excellent way to discreetly arm pro-American forces for the CIA's secret wars.

Unlike Laos and Nicaragua, in Jamaica there was no civil war. The CIA still found a way to exploit the political climate with the armed conflict between PNP and JLP supporters.

---

24 Tom Fawthrop, Vang Pao Obituary (The Guardian, 2011) http://www.theguardian.com/world/2011/feb/22/vang-pao-obituary

25 Contras, Cocaine And Covert Operations (National Security Archive George Washington University) http://nsarchive.gwu.edu/NSAEBB/NSAEBB2/index.html

The JLP supporters already had experience in low-level arms conflicts and drug smuggling from the marijuana trade. It is not a stretch to believe that the CIA would use the drug trade to arm JLP gunmen in their fight against Michael Manley, who the U.S. feared would make Jamaica a Communist country.

Several armed JLP supporters, including Lester "Jim Brown" Coke and Vivian Blake, went on to become big players in the cocaine trade. Others like Cecil Connor aka Charles Little Nut Miller and Richard "Storyteller" Morrison would admit that the CIA helped them become the powerful criminals they were before being eventually incarcerated.

The Cubans of Brigade 2506, many of whom went on to become involved in Operation 40, were another group of right-wing militants involved in the cocaine trade. Many Cubans would enter the cocaine trade with training from, or while still working with, the CIA. The training in weapons, assassinations, smuggling, flying, bombings, and spying made these trained Cubans very powerful gangsters who were able to leverage their connections in Latin America and the U.S. to become major players in the cocaine trade.

Michael Manley would speak of a plot by the Mafia and Jamaicans in Miami to turn Jamaica into a hub for hard drugs and connect it to the plan to destabilize Jamaica. After Seaga defeated Manley in the 1980 election, Jamaica would go on to become a major center for Colombian cocaine being exported to the U.S.

During the 1980s, the cocaine trade exploded and under Seaga's control, Lester "Jim Brown " Coke and the JLP's armed faction the Shower Posse would become major players in the import and distribution of cocaine into the United States. The fact that his bodyguard and enforcer had become a millionaire drug kingpin would have been something impossible for Seaga not to notice. Brown had been running guns into Jamaica since at least 1979, when a retired U.S. agent would say:

> Jim Brown was buying guns like they were going out of fashion. He was coming into the U.S. on a visa, and he had plenty of money. You think it was Jim Brown's money he was spending to bring back guns to Jamaica that were used to kill the opposition? Give me a break. Where did the money come from? Use your imagination on that one.[26]

The guns that Jim Brown would bring into Jamaica would lead to Jamaica having one of the most violent elections ever: 844 people were murdered, many due to political violence. The election again would coincide with the American election, with the right wing winning strongly and putting in office hardcore anti-Communist Ronald Reagan. Reagan's vice president was George H.W. Bush, who had run the CIA while it was destabilizing Jamaica in the previous election in 1976.

Seaga would stay true to the anti-Cuban, pro-American stance he had taken in the 1976 election and would expel the Cuban ambassador, later breaking all ties with Cuba. He would be rewarded with a dramatic increase in aid from the United States and would be the first foreign dignitary to visit the White House after Reagan's election.

Seaga would become Reagan's man in the West Indies, helping create the Caribbean Basin Initiative (CBI), which opened Jamaica and other countries to private business. Some would claim it also led to the exploitation of the Caribbean by American business. This initiative was intended to wipe out some of the leftist and Communist movements in the Caribbean

---

26 Charles Miller Vs. U.S. Department Of Justice https://archive.org/stream/gov.uscourts.dcd.115892/gov.uscourts.dcd.115892.14.1_djvu.txt

as well. Seaga would also help lead the charge when America invaded the country of Grenada, which recently had had a coup and was strengthening ties with Cuba.

Aside from the aid that Seaga would receive from the U.S. and the IMF, it appears he also benefitted from the cocaine trade. During the 1980s, the Reagan administration would have close ties with people involved in the cocaine trade from the Colombian Cali and Medellin cartels, Manuel Noriega, and the Contras, in order to further their right-wing agenda and the war on Communism.

Seaga's connections to the cocaine trade did not end with Lester "Jim Brown" Coke, his bodyguard, political enforcer, major player in the cocaine trade, and Don of Seaga's JLP stronghold Tivoli Gardens. In 1983, Seaga would start a partnership with Eli Tisona, an Israeli businessman who was also a known mobster. The partnership was supposed to be an agricultural venture in which Tisona would invest in fruits and vegetables being transported from Jamaica to the United States and Europe.

Tisona had no experience in agriculture except for running a Wimpies burger chain in Israel. According to Jamaican journalist Mark Wignall, two of Seaga's ministers had told him that they received information from Israeli officials that Tisona was an Israeli mobster, while they were working together. According to Wignall, Tisona's planes would fly from Colombia to Jamaica where they would pick up winter vegetables before flying to the United States and Europe, making it an ideal front for cocaine smuggling. According to the *Miami Sun-Sentinel*, Tisona would sell his share in the company after his partner was busted for selling drugs from the operation out of fish crates[27]. Author

---

27   Mark Wignall, Seaga Can Not Have It Both Ways (Jamaica Observer, 2010)   http://www.jamaicaobserver.com/columns/

Thomas Feiling would claim that Tisona would use notorious Jamaican drug dealer, Lester "Jim Brown" Coke as head of security for one of his "farms.[28]"

In 1997, the Israeli government named Eli Tisona and his brother the two top crime figures in the country. In 1999, Tisona would be convicted in Florida for laundering more than $42 million of cocaine money for the Cali Cartel over a two-year period[29]. Tisona also owned a fish farm in Bogota, Colombia, with partner Phanor Arizabaleta, a leader of the Cali Cartel. This was another Tisona business which made an ideal front for drug trafficking. Tisona would also use his jewelry business to launder cash made from cocaine sales.

Tisona was found guilty of 146 charges related to money laundering and sentenced to 19 years in prison. The case was one of the biggest drug money laundering cases in the history of United States. While there is no evidence that Tisona was involved in cocaine trafficking while he was in Jamaica, it would not be hard to believe he was not using his operation in Jamaica to smuggle drugs and launder drug money.

Tisona was not the only Israeli involved in the Latin American and Caribbean drug trade. Manuel Noriega's right hand man in Panama was a Mossad (Israeli intelligence) agent and Oliver North's partner in the Iran-Cocaine-Contra was a Mossad agent named Amiram Nir.

In 1988, Senator John Kerry would hold hearings on international drug trafficking due to media reports connecting the American-supported Contras to cocaine trafficking. Kerry

---

Seaga-cannot-have-it-both-ways_7721762

28 Thomas Feiling, *Cocaine Nation: How the White Trade Took Over the World* (Pegasus, 2012)

29 Associated Press, Alleged Israeli Mobster Convicted (1999) http://www.apnewsarchive.com/1999/Alleged-Israeli-Mobster-Convicted/id-633092287d97f4518a5bec782071c281

would interview several veterans of the drug trade about their connections to the Contras, Panamanian ruler Manuel Noriega, and American intelligence agencies.

Two drug dealers who testified were Michael Palmer and Michael Vogel. Palmer was a known marijuana trafficker who ran Vortex Air, which imported massive amounts of marijuana from Colombia to the United States. Palmer wound up involved in the Iran-Contra scandal after it was revealed that Palmer worked with Oliver North to supply the Contras with humanitarian aide and had received $96,000 from the state department for his services. The humanitarian aid was, in fact, guns being flown in and drugs being flown out of Central America.

Palmer was also under the full protection of the government, so when he got indicted for cocaine trafficking in Detroit, the DEA was able to cover for him, claiming he was an informant. While Palmer ran the importation end of the marijuana and cocaine organization in the U.S., his partner Michael Vogel handled distribution.

Vogel would testify about the international drug trade to Congress. He would bring up Jamaica and how it was used as a hub for drug traffickers and how officials there were bought off. Vogel would testify that he felt completely safe in Jamaica and that he was sure the Seaga government was aware of and condoned the narcotics trafficking on the island.

According to Vogel, a good deal of money was transferred from Jamaica to the Cayman Islands, a country well known for money laundering due to its lax banking laws. Vogel claimed that Seaga was a prime beneficiary of the money being laundered from Jamaica to the Caymans, that Seaga was in control of the

Cayman capital of Georgetown and that his brother owned property on the Cayman Islands worth $38 million.[30]

Seaga has never been convicted of a crime, but his ties to drug dealers and the high rate of cocaine, marijuana, and weapons that came through Jamaica during the 80s when the CIA was freely using the drug trade to fund right-wing dictators, armies, militias, and political parties are enough to raise eyebrows and questions.

---

30 Mike Vogel's Testimony To The Kerry Committee (CSPAN-1988) http://www.c-span.org/video/?2096-1/drug-control-central-america-day-2

CHAPTER 9

A FORMER CIA AGENT COMES TO JAMAICA

On September 9, 1976, the anti-CIA forces in Jamaica pulled off a daring attack against the CIA by inviting Philip Agee, a former CIA agent turned whistleblower to speak in the country.

Agee joined the CIA in 1958 and worked in Mexico, Uruguay, and Ecuador. In 1969, after realizing that the CIA was not fighting for democracy but was in fact causing great harm to the countries it was involved in, Agee left the agency and wrote a book about his experiences.

In his book *Inside the Company: CIA Diary*, Agee claimed that while in Ecuador, he would use bribes, illegal surveillance recordings, forgery, and intimidation to try and harm Ecuador's relationship with Cuba. He would also detail the CIA's support for military dictatorships and their death squads used to subdue opposing political groups, the assassinations and torture the CIA was involved in, as well as their manipulation of the press.

Agee would also expose more than 250 CIA agents and officers, including the presidents of Costa Rica, Mexico, and Colombia. Due to his actions, he was called a traitor by CIA head George H.W. Bush and became a nemesis of Ted Shackley, who was Deputy Director of Operations under Bush in 1976.

Agee would come to Jamaica at the request of leftist political activist and professor Trevor Munroe and his Workers Liberation League. Agee would give an interview with the Jamaica Broadcasting Corporation (JBC) on September 10, in which he claimed that the American Embassy had an office for the CIA and that there were at least two CIA agents working under nonofficial cover.

Soon after, the normally anti-Manley *Jamaica Gleaner* ran a reprint of an article by Saul Landau that originally ran in *The Washington Post*, accusing the CIA of destabilizing Jamaica. Another newspaper, *Public Opinion*, ran the same story on their front page. Landau worked closely with Orlando Letelier, a Chilean Socialist killed by CIA-trained terrorists Luis Posada, Orlando Bosch, and their underlings. *The Jamaica Daily News* published an article "How the CIA Cracked Allende", which talked about the CIA-supported military coup in Chile.

Agee conducted a number of interviews on government-run radio and television. In these interviews, he would discuss the economic destabilization and manipulation of the press. He'd also compare what was going on in Jamaica to what had happened in Chile before that. He told *Jamaican Broadcast Radio*:

> I don't know anything regarding the specifics of what limited official use they would be doing here but I do know they have an office here in the U.S. Embassy and they undoubtedly have a few people; 2 3 maybe, under non official cover, i.e., as businessmen, tourists, retired people, whatever, and that they undoubtedly are active. They are not sitting around here clipping newspapers and looking at the ceiling. They are an activist organization by definition. Remember that the CIA is not the only agency involved, there are

others too and they were in Chile too as you probably know if you have seen that Chile report, so that the CIA is only one agency active in this sort of thing and they get involved in the dirty work and the secret activities. There is the department of the treasury, there are commercial banks, there are all sorts of agencies, which also have a role to play in what has become known as destabilization because of the Chile incident. So there are very strong indicators. We know there is a CIA office here. I think you can draw certain conclusions to that.[31]

Agee claimed that while he had no hard evidence or documents that the CIA was involved in Jamaica, from his days as a CIA officer he knew the two previous Station Chiefs who ran operations in Jamaica, Jack Kaufman and Tom Keenan. Agee would go on to allege that the CIA had an office on the third floor of the American Embassy in Kingston. The First National Bank of New York, which had several branches in Kingston, was often used by the CIA and was very active in Kingston, and Agee also said the CIA might be using missionaries and businessmen as agents.

While Agee did not bring up the issue of guns, U.S. Ambassador Sumner Gerard would make a primer on alleged destabilization and his allegations included that guns were part of the so-called destabilization effort that was being lobbied at U.S. agencies and interests.

Guns are smuggled into Jamaica to keep the level of violence up, and to arm the government's opposition. The alleged sources for these weapons are the Mafia,

---

31 US Embassy In Jamaica Cable (PHILIP AGEE'S ALLEGATIONS RE CIA AND DESTABILIZATION OF JAMAICA) https://wikileaks.org/plusd/cables/1976KINGST03873_b.html

perhaps in alliance with anti-Manley forces in the Jamaican community in the U.S., and by implication the USG (U.S. Government) and the multinationals.[32]

Manley would tie in the use of guns without calling out the CIA by name. In a speech on September 21 at the annual PNP Conference, Manley referred to "a clique who were determined to halt Jamaica's progress toward democratic socialism. To do so, the clique has taken over the JLP (no a "yo'yo"), and let loose upon Jamaica... vicious propaganda, adopted a strategy of guns and violence, and undertaken economic sabotage.[33]"

Clearly the clique that Manley was talking about was the CIA and the JLP. Still, Manley did not bring up Agee's allegations during his speech, despite the fact that it happened right after Agee's visit.

At a meeting at the YWCA Hall in Jamaica, Agee claimed that the CIA was working with people opposed to the government to perform their dirty tricks for them and that they would bribe government, army, and police officials for information and subversive acts.

Agee went on to name several people he claimed were working for the CIA out of the American Embassy: Norman Descoteaux and his wife, Judy; Joel Beyer; Dan Calloway; Jerzy Hauptmann; James Holt; Brian Bennett; Ken Stanton; and Adrienne Mackenzie. Holt had met several times with Michael Manley's spy Albert Robinson and was at the center of many of the allegations of CIA interference in Jamaica.

---

32 US Embassy In Jamaica Cable (A PRIMER ON DESTABILIZATION IN JAMAICA) https://search.wikileaks.org/plusd/cables/1978KINGST08634_d.html

33 US Embassy In Jamaica Cable (PNP HOLDS ANNUAL CONFERENCE) https://www.wikileaks.org/plusd/cables/1976KINGST04062_b.html

Agee claimed that he knew Norman Descoteaux from the CIA when Descoteaux was working for the CIA in Guayaquil, Ecuador. In a press release, Agee outlined the method he used for identifying the CIA agents as well as gave their roles both for the CIA and for the embassy. He would also give the addresses, telephone numbers, and vehicles used by the CIA agents. This information was used in anti-CIA leaflets that were distributed throughout Kingston with the following note:

> Unless these persons can satisfy us that they are not CIA agents, they must leave. We want good relations with all countries. We want good relations with America. But we don't want their spies. Let the CIA mind their own business and go back to America. Leave Jamaicans to run our own affairs.[34]

Most of the alleged CIA agents fled Jamaica after Agee called them out. Research shows that most of the people named by Agee were, in fact, CIA agents, and many now list the CIA on their resumes and talk about their experiences with the organization openly.

While it seems pretty clear that Manley was involved in bringing Agee to Jamaica, due to the use of government-sponsored radio and television, Manley would not use Agee's allegations in the lead-up to the upcoming election in 1976. If Manley wanted to prove that the CIA was involved in Jamaica, he had information from the bombing attempt in July of Cuban Flight 455 at the airport named after his father, Norman Manley, that implicated anti-Castro Cubans affiliated with the CIA. Manley would have also known that these same CIA-trained

---

34 US Embassy In Jamaica Cable (LEAFLETS IDENTIFYING ALLEGED CIA AGENTS BEING SCATTERED THROUGHOUT KINGSTON) https:// wikileaks.org/plusd/cables/1976STATE232018_b.html

terrorists would wind up blowing up the same plane four months later, killing 73 innocent civilians.

Manley's friend Fidel Castro would directly charge the CIA with involvement in the plane bombing. At the funeral for the victims of the bombing, Castro would say, The CIA had directly organized the sabotage. Despite the fact that the bombing was not only an act of terrorism against Cuba but the Caribbean as a whole, Manley was quiet on the subject. A cable sent from Ambassador Sumner Gerard hints at the reasons for Manley not directly charging the CIA with terrorizing and destabilizing Jamaica.

> The U.S. is not among the winners. The destabilization-CIA theme was loudly played in the early stages of the campaign and although muted in the final movement, was still there as a leit-motif. It will be seen as having been an effective local political theme and may be expected to be re-played whenever a diversion from reality is required. The confirmed reason for the recent muting is the expectation of the Manley government of substantial goodies from the Carter administration.[35]

Manley was in a tough position. He clearly wanted the CIA out of Jamaica but wanted to remain on good terms with the United States. It seems evident that Manley was receiving intelligence from Cuba about the CIA and their Cuban terrorist hitmen. Agee's long history of exposing the CIA has been attacked but not discredited. It is unlikely that Agee would waste his time or credibility in Jamaica if there weren't a large-scale CIA operation there.

---

35   US Embassy In Jamaica Cable (MANLEY'S RE-ELECTION: IMPLICATIONS FOR U.S) https://search.wikileaks.org/plusd/cables/1976KINGST05459_b.html

CHAPTER 10

DID THE CIA TRY AND KILL BOB MARLEY?

One incident that has caused a great deal of speculation about CIA involvement was the shooting of Bob Marley on December 3, 1976. At the request of PNP Minister of Housing Tony Spaulding, Marley had agreed to play a concert called Smile Jamaica on December 5th. Spaulding had set up a house for Marley's family in Bull Bay, far away from Kingston where Marley was staying in an upper class area, 56 Hope Road. After Marley agreed to do the concert for Spaulding, Manley called for elections ten days after the concert. The date of the concert also coincided with the release of Edward Seaga's new JLP Manifesto.

Marley had even recorded a song of the same name for the concert, "Smile Jamaica," an upbeat, positive song about being in Jamaica. The upbeat message stood in dark contrast to the levels of political violence that were plaguing Kingston in 1976. He agreed to do the show on the conditions that it wasn't political, but it appeared he was betrayed by Manley and Spaulding. Spaulding was helpful to Marley, getting the reggae star some of his first shows in New York City in the early 70s, and Marley had performed at PNP rallies in the states.

A month before the concert, a JLP motorcade was fired on in York Town. Nine people were shot and several buildings, including the PNP headquarters, were burned down. Seaga was in the motorcade but was not near the shooting.

Marley was not involved in Jamaican politics and had friends on both sides. Claudie Massop, Seaga's right hand man and the ranking Don of Tivoli Gardens, was close with Marley and considered him a friend, as did Tony Welch, Tony Spaulding's enforcer in Arnett Gardens. Welch, who went by the name Red Tony, ran a sound system called Socialist Roots, connecting reggae and Rastafarianism to the PNP. Massop was in jail at the time but wrote a letter to Marley discouraging him from performing at the concert.

People from both political parties took Marley's "Smile Jamaica" song and concert as an endorsement for the PNP. After years of working hard in Jamaica, Bob Marley was finally becoming an international celebrity and was given all the money, fame, and power that came with it. At the time, Bob Marley's live version of "No Woman No Cry" was his breakthrough international hit. Both sides saw the concert as an event that could shift the election into Manley's favor.

While Bob Marley had not taken sides between the PNP and the JLP, he had clearly taken a side against the CIA and the power it represented. Marley's 1974 album *Natty Dread* included the songs, "Them Belly Full" and "Revolution."

The first song, "Them Belly Full," was about the inequity between the poor and the rich and the frustration and anger it creates. The second song, "Revolution," talked about changing the system and freeing political prisoners. The song also warned against letting politicians do you favors, a lesson Marley did not heed when he allowed Tony Spaulding to get his family housing.

In 1975, Bob Marley released his massively successful *Live!* album. The album contained a live versions of his song "Get Up, Stand Up," an anthem for poor and oppressed people fighting against their oppressors, and the anti-authority "I Shot The Sheriff," which became a Billboard number-one hit in America by Eric Clapton. Another song included was "Burnin and Lootin," another anthem for poor people rising up against the system.

These songs posed a threat to the CIA, not only in Jamaica but in the whole world. Bob Marley's message for poor people to rise up against their oppressors was troubling to the CIA, whose main agenda was to keep governments that oppressed poor people up and running in the name of capitalism.

Rastaman Vibration was released in April of 1976 and was one of Marley's most politically charged albums. One song, "Crazy Baldhead," was critical of the Jamaican upper class and its treatment of Rastafarians and poor people. Another song, "War," was taken from a speech Haile Selassie gave at the United Nations. The song claims that war is caused by racism and calls for the end of first-class and second-class citizens, and for basic human rights for everyone in the world. In the song, Marley called out the ignoble and unhappy regimes of Angola and South Africa. The CIA at the time was very much involved with South Africa fighting a war in Angola and had been giving support for South Africa, having helped South African police capture Nelson Mandela.

Marley called out the CIA by name in the song, "Rat Race." In the song he said, "Political violence fills your city/Don't involve Rasta in your sese (gossip)/Rasta no work for no CIA." These lyrics can be interpreted in part as blaming the CIA for the political violence in Kingston, and also as distancing himself from the JLP, who were being connected to the CIA at the time.

Bob Marley was heavily influenced by Marcus Garvey, a Jamaican who had started an organization called the United Negro Improvement Association (UNIA). Garvey intensely preached Black pride and unity and wanted to take Black people back to Africa. He had four million members in his organization and in 1920, J. Edgar Hoover of the FBI targeted Garvey and he was deported back to Jamaica.

In 1969, the CIA published a memo, "Black Radicalism in the Caribbean," in which they discussed their fear of the Black Power Movement migrating from the States to the West Indies. The memo discussed how Black U.S. leaders like Stokely Carmichael and H. Rap Brown were banned from Jamaica by the JLP leadership and how they made attempts to discredit Black Power figures like Walter Rodney. Rodney, who spoke out against imperialism, America, and racism, was originally from Guyana but was a lecturer at the University of the West Indies in Jamaica. JLP Prime Minister Hugh Shearer, who blamed Rodney for planning a Castro-like takeover of Jamaica, would later kick Rodney out of the country[36].

The CIA also kept a close eye on Robert Hill, a Jamaican associate of Rodney's, who was also heavily influenced by Marcus Garvey. The CIA was fearful that the Black Power or Black Nationalist Movements in the Caribbean would get co-opted by the Communists and Cubans. The CIA also was keeping track of the Rastafarians as they became more politicized.

So after already making himself an enemy of the CIA through his music, Marley also made an enemy of the JLP by agreeing to perform at a concert organized by the PNP during a time of fierce political and street war between the two parties.

---

36 Black Radicalism In The Caribbean (CIA Memo, 1969) http://www.foia.cia.gov/sites/default/files/document_conversions/89801/DOC_0000927143.pdf

At 8:30 p.m., on December 3, 1976, two days before the Smile Jamaica concert and 12 days before the election in Jamaica, upward of seven men with guns came into Marley's house at 56 Hope Road. Marley and his band were on break from rehearsing and Marley's wife, Rita, was shot in the head while in her car. The gunmen proceeded to the kitchen where Marley, his manager Don Taylor, and several other people in his band and entourage were gathered.

A shot grazed Marley's chest and stuck in his arm. Don Taylor was shot in the legs and torso. Nancy Burke, Marley's next-door neighbor and friend, recalled hearing his percussionist and close friend, Alvin "Seeco" Patterson, say, "Blood claat! Is Seaga men! Dem come fi kill Bob!" There were also numerous reports that after the shooting, the gunmen headed to the JLP stronghold of Tivoli Gardens[37].

Laurie Gunst, who wrote *Born Fi' Dead* that covers much of the history of political violence, claims that Trevor Philips, who was the chairman of the 1978 Peace Concert, was told by Marley that Lester "Jim Brown" Coke, Seaga's bodyguard, was involved in the attempt on his life. After the shooting, a cable was sent from the American Embassy entitled *Reggae Star Shot: Motive probably political.* The cable from Ambassador Gerard read:

> Some see the incident as an attempt by JLP gunmen to halt the concert, which would feature the "politically progressive" music of Marley and other reggae stars. Others see it as a deep-laid plot to create a progressive, youthful Jamaican martyr to the benefit of the PNP. Those holding the latter view note that of the four persons shot, three of them including Marley

---

37 Vivien Goldman, *Book Of Exodus* (Random House New York) 108.

suffered only minor wounds. Too, the assailants may simply be enemies of Marley or one of his associates. Whatever the cause, the incident will be with us for some time, given Marley's popularity. Contributing to this view is the fact that, while the newspapers have given the shooting prominent coverage, the reporting has been curiously uninformative.

Timothy White, author of the definitive Marley biography *Catch a Fire*, claimed that information he received from JLP and PNP officials as well as U.S. law enforcement officials led him to believe that Carl Byah "Mitchell," a JLP gunman, was contracted by the CIA to organize the Marley shooting and that Lester "Jim Brown" Coke led the charge on Hope Road.[38]

Don Taylor, Marley's manager, would claim that both he and Marley were present at a ghetto court in which the gunmen who shot Marley were captured and later executed. Before one of the shooters was killed, Taylor claims that shooter admitted doing the job for the CIA in return for cocaine and guns[39].

Another Marley biographer, Jon Masouri, claims that Marley and Don Taylor met with Michael Manley in London after the shooting, and Manley indicated he'd uncovered evidence that the CIA was involved in the shooting[40].

If the CIA was trying to silence Marley and harm Manley's chances at winning the election, they failed miserably. Marley's wounds would prevent him from playing guitar, but not from performing. He was introduced by Michael Manley at the Smile Jamaica Concert, and would perform "War," a song protesting against the colonial interests that the CIA represented. Manley

---

38 Timothy White, *Catch A Fire* (Holt Rinehart And Winston, New York)
39 Don Taylor, *Marley And Me* (Barricade Books, New Jersey)
40 Jon Masouri, *Wailing Blues - The Story of Bob Marley's Wailers* (Omnibus Press, New York)

was perched on top of a van surrounded by ghetto gunmen, in a symbol of triumph. Both men were winners: the shooting had helped Marley gain mythic and legendary status, and Manley was able to have an epic concert that would boost him going into the upcoming elections.

Marley addressed the shootings in songs including "Ambush in the Night," where he blamed the Jamaican system of corrupt politics for his shooting and in "Time Will Tell," where he sang: "Lock them up, not the brothers/but the ones who set them up."

Marley maintained ties with both the PNP and the JLP. Marley was good friends with Claudie Massop, and the two would speak about starting their own political party in Jamaica. Marley would also become friends with Vivian Blake, one of the leaders of the Shower Posse.

Massop and PNP Don Bucky Marshall would ask Marley to perform at a concert to bring peace between the two warring political parties. Marley would bring together Edward Seaga and Michael Manley on stage a year and a half after he had been shot before the Smile Jamaica concert.

As powerful as Bob Marley was, he could not stop the cycle of political violence that had been fueled by the CIA. Within two years, the two organizers of the concert, Bucky Marshall and Claudie Massop, were killed and the 1980 election between Seaga and Manley would be the most violent election in Jamaica's history.

CHAPTER 11

HOW THE CIA CREATED THE JAMAICAN SHOWER POSSE

One of the most common allegations against the CIA in Jamaica is that of its connection to organized crime, drugs, and guns. The CIA has a long history of collaborating with criminals and drug dealers. This started with the CIA's predecessor: the Office of Strategic Services (OSS) and Charles "Lucky" Luciano. Intelligence officers contacted infamous crime figure Meyer Lansky to arrange a meeting with Lucky Luciano during World War II. The OSS used Lansky and Luciano to recruit informants from the docks on the east coast, which the Mafia controlled. The OSS named their operation Operation Underworld. The OSS also used Luciano's Italian Mafia connections to get information before their invasion of Italy in World War II.[41]

During the Cold War, the CIA would continue to use the Mafia to help them fight Castro. The CIA would admit to collaborating with Mafia members such as Johnny Roselli and drug kingpin Santo Trafficante to try to assassinate Castro. There is a great

---

41 Eric Umansky, History 101: The CIA & Drugs (Mother Jones, 1998) http://www.motherjones.com/politics/1998/06/history-101-cia-drugs

deal of testimony and evidence that the CIA also worked with the Mafia to have Kennedy assassinated.[42]

During 1976, a year which would become a big turning point in Jamaica for drugs and violence, the CIA was run by George H.W. Bush. Bush later ran the secret war in Nicaragua, in which the CIA and other government officials helped the Contras import cocaine into the U.S. to fund their war against the Sandinista government. George Bush's number two, Ted Shackley, was Deputy Director of Operations in 1976. Shackley was in charge of CIA operations in Laos, where the CIA was involved in helping General Vang Pao's heroin-running operation. Shackley was very close to Bush, and Shackley's wife worked on Bush's presidential campaign in 1980 and later became involved with Bush in the Iran-Contra scandal.

Jamaica would prove itself to be an ideal place to be exploited by the CIA. Although it did not have a rebel force or military that the CIA could use to overthrow Manley's leftist government with force, Seaga's gunmen would prove to be an ideal paramilitary source. Jamaicans also had a good deal of experience smuggling marijuana, so the CIA's tactic of supporting political groups by enabling them in the drug trade was an easy fit.

Jamaica also was an ideal location for both the gun and drug trades, located 500 miles from Miami and 1,000 miles from Colombia. When Castro took over Cuba, the other Caribbean islands would become all the more valuable in the drug trade.

Just as Jamaica's location made it an ideal place for the slave and sugar trade in the 18th century, it was an ideal place for the guns and drug trade in the 1970s. With thousands of Jamaican immigrants in the U.S., the U.K., and Canada, and a long history of Jamaicans smuggling marijuana into the United

---

42 Robert D. Morrow, *First Hand Knowledge: How I Participated in the CIA - Mafia Murder of President Kennedy* (SPI Books, 1993)

States and other countries, Jamaica would be an ideal point for drug shipments.

In several speeches, Manley spoke of a Mafia attempt to transform Jamaica into a hub for hard drugs, often connecting it to the CIA's destabilization efforts.[43] Peter Whittingham, a JLP political candidate arrested by Manley's forces for allegedly planning a coup to oust Manley from power, was arrested in Miami for importing more than two million dollars worth of marijuana[44]. The Mafia that Manley referred to was Santo Trafficante and the Miami Cubans, who had a near monopoly of the cocaine trade in the 1970s.

In May of 1974, a plane carrying drugs from Jamaica to Miami was shot down. The Jamaican government claimed that the operation behind the plane was trafficking not only marijuana grown in Jamaica, but heroin and cocaine as well. The government also claimed that several small planes involved in drug smuggling had been seized and that 50 American citizens involved in the operation had been arrested. Three months later, Minister of National Security Eli Matalon, who was leading the charge to stop the drug trade in Jamaica, had a grenade placed in his car while visiting the DEA office in Miami.[45]

Just as many of the CIA trained anti-Castro Cubans from Brigade 2506 and Operation 40 would go on to become big players in the international drug trade, so would many of Seaga's forces of anti-Manley gunmen.

---

43 US Embassy In Jamaica Cable (GOJ BUDGET DEBATE - MANLEY URGES END TO "DESTABILIZATION") https://search.wikileaks.org/plusd/cables/1976KINGST01941_b.html

44 The Struggle, 1977 http://ufdc.ufl.edu/UF00100337/00039

45 Prime Minister Thanks Agency (Associated Press, 1976) https://news.google.com/newspapers?nid=1346&dat=19740821&id=M-4vAAAAIBAJ&sjid=AvsDAAAAIBAJ&pg=5621,5683134&hl=en

Many gangsters from Edward Seaga's JLP stronghold of Tivoli Gardens achieved the notoriety and infamy usually reserved for American Mafia figures. This group was called The Shower Posse. Some claim that it was named after a Seaga speech in which he promised to shower his constituency with gifts. Others claim it was after its members, who showered their victims with bullets.

Claudie Massop was the Don of Tivoli for most of the 70s, but he was killed in 1979, less than a year after organizing the One Love peace concert. His replacement was Lester Lloyd Coke, who carried the nickname Jim Brown after the famous American football star and action movie hero.

Lester Lloyd "Jim Brown" Coke was not only Tivoli Gardens's Don, but he also served as Edward Seaga's bodyguard. Coke wound up being charged with several murders in both Jamaica and the U.S., where he would also face cocaine trafficking charges. But before he could face trial in America, he was burned to death in his cell in Jamaica in a murder that remains unsolved.

One close cohort of Lester Coke was Richard "Storyteller" Morrison, who was indicted along with Coke on murder and drug charges in Miami. Morrison told fellow prisoner Anthony Prince that he had flown millions of dollars worth of guns and drugs between Colombia, Miami, and Jamaica. He would also tell Prince that the U.S. government turned a blind eye to the Shower Posse in the early 80s and that the CIA had all but assisted in the trafficking of weapons, with Seaga supporting the American government in the overthrow of Grenadian Prime Minister Maurice Bishop. Prince would refer to the Shower Posse as not only a violent gang but also a counter-revolutionary paramilitary force employed by the JLP to destabilize the PNP and would refer to Morrison as someone who had helped overthrow a government in Jamaica.[46]

Morrison showed Prince pictures of the many luxury cars he owned and told him about helicopters, airplanes, and property in Florida and Jamaica. Prince would also say that once the Shower Posse was no longer useful to the U.S. government, Morrison and his boss Lester Coke were extradited to face charges for the activities condoned by the CIA, and that Coke's knowledge of the Shower Posse's involvement with the CIA and the JLP died with him when he was burned alive in his cell.

Another prominent figure in the Shower Posse was Cecil Connor. Born in St. Kitts, Connor would immigrate to Jamaica, where he aligned himself with Edward Seaga's Tivoli Garden militia.

Connor wound up testifying against his former cohorts Lester "Jim Brown" Coke and Vivian Blake, the leaders of the Shower Posse. He claimed that he worked for the underworld section of the JLP and that he stuffed ballot boxes and intimidated voters in order to make sure the Seaga and the JLP retained their power in the government.

He also said that as a member of the Shower Posse, he smuggled marijuana and cocaine from Jamaica to Florida, laundered drug money, and attended gangland executions. Connor testified in court that he was present when Lester Coke and other Shower Posse members opened fire at a Miami crackhouse, killing five people including a pregnant woman, and was involved in several drug-related murders[47].

Connor also claimed in several interviews that while working with the Shower Posse, he was a CIA operative. He told

46 Anthony Prince, Bank Robbery For Beginners (Macmillan, New York)
47 Charles Miller Vs. U.S. Department Of Justice https://archive.org/stream/gov.uscourts.dcd.115892/gov.uscourts.dcd.115892.14.1_djvu.txt

Newsweek that the CIA trained him in spying and killing; that America made him who he was and that the CIA trained him how to make bombs and kill people with his watch.

Via UPI, Connor said, "I was used by the Americans originally in Jamaica and all the politics stuff there in Miami, and I just don't want to talk about it & is people like me help mash-up socialism in Jamaica." According to reports, Connor admitted to killing and intimidating leftist opponents of Edward Seaga with secret U.S. help.

The New York Times reported that Connor also claimed that the CIA helped break him out of prison in Jamaica, where he was serving a 75-year sentence for armed robbery and assault with the intent to kill.[48]

After testifying against Shower Posse leaders Vivian Blake, Lester Coke, and Richard "Storyteller" Morrison in 1989, Connor entered the witness protection program and changed his name to Charles Miller, becoming the manager of a Domino's Pizza franchise in Maine. Soon he would return to the Caribbean island of St. Kitts, where he was born and raised, with an American passport.

In St. Kitts, Connor returned to his old games with a new name, earning the new nickname "Little Nut." On his native island, Charles "Little Nut" Miller would continue working in the drug trade, using the skills he learned from the CIA and the Shower Posse.

Connor was eventually charged by the United States for importing more than half a ton of cocaine from St. Kitts to Miami in 1995. Connor threatened to kill American medical

---

48 Larry Rohter, A Turncoat Now Turning On Americans In Caribbean (The New York Times, 1998) http://www.nytimes.com/1998/08/23/world/a-turncoat-now-turning-on-americans-in-caribbean.html

students at Ross University in St. Kitts if there was an attempt to extradite him.

When Connor was eventually extradited to America in 2000, he faced trial and was convicted for the same drug conspiracy charges he testified against his former Shower Posse cohorts. At his trial, a former colleague of his would accuse him of killing the Deputy Prime Minister's son and his girlfriend over a missing cocaine shipment.

During Lester "Jim Brown" Coke's funeral, Edward Seaga led the procession, honoring his bodyguard and political enforcer, who also happened to be a cocaine kingpin. In an interview at the funeral, Seaga said Coke was "a protector of the community."[49] While Jim Brown may have been a protector and supporter for the thousands of residents in Tivoli Gardens and other JLP constituencies where he provided food, clothing, and other necessities, to the police and constituencies not loyal to the JLP, he was a mass murderer and a terrorist.

Coke not only terrorized Jamaica, but Miami as well and caught the attention of U.S. drug agents. A retired U.S. law enforcement agent who knew of Lester "Jim Brown" Coke's activities in Jamaica said:

> In 1982, Jim Brown got into a traffic accident with a bus driver in Denham Town in Jamaica. The driver would run for safety to the Denham Town police station but the police, knowledgeable of Brown's reputation did nothing and Brown and his cohorts dragged him out of the station and shot and stabbed him to death. After bus drivers went on strike to protest the killing, the police would lock up Lester Coke and charge him with

---

49 'Jim Brown' Is Still Dead, Isn't He? (Newsweek, 1992) http://www.newsweek.com/jim-brown-still-dead-isnt-he-197434

murder, but he would be set free after no witnesses would testify against him.

In May of 1984, Jim Brown led a troop of armed men from Tivoli Gardens to nearby Rema, where people had been complaining that their neighborhood had been neglected by the ruling JLP. Brown and company burned down several houses, killing 22 people, in what Jamaican police called an act of terrorism. Brown was extradited from Miami to Jamaica for those charges but once again, due to his political connections and intimidation of witnesses, he was set free.

U.S. authorities would claim that the Shower Posse, led by Jim Brown in Tivoli and Vivian Blake in the U.S., were responsible for more than 1,400 murders, the casualty toll of a small civil war. The Associated Press would claim that in the 80s, Jamaican drug gangs controlled 40 percent of the American crack cocaine market. In 1988, 120 Shower Posse members from 20 different states were arrested on gun and drug smuggling and conspiracy charges.[50]

Eventually, when Michael Manley came back into power, Jim Brown would be arrested in Jamaica but would be burned alive in his cell before he could face trial. In many ways, the Shower Posse mirrored the CIA-trained Brigade 2506 of Cubans, who would go on to commit acts of terrorism and become major players in the cocaine trade. The claims of the CIA's involvement with the Shower Posse are backed up by a pattern of CIA involvement in the drug trade and connections to criminal organizations across the world.

---

50 Associated Press, U.S. Captures 120 In Gang Roundup (The New York Times, 1988) http://www.nytimes.com/1988/10/14/us/us-captures-120-in-gang-roundup.html

CHAPTER 12

THE CIA AND TERRORISM IN THE CARIBBEAN

While America has claimed to have wars on terrorism and drugs, the CIA's support of Luis Posada Carilles has shown its utmost hypocrisy. On October 6, 1976, Cuban Aviation Flight 455 blew up over the ocean while flying from Barbados to Jamaica. Freddy Lugo and Hernan Ricardo Lozano, two employees of Luis Posada Carilles, placed a bomb on the plane. Orlando Bosch and Posada would take credit for the bombing in several interviews. The bombing of the plane resulted in the deaths of 73 civilians, including 24 members of the Cuban fencing team and 11 Guyanese medical students.

Bosch and Posada were arrested for the crime and both wound up serving several years in jail in Venezuela. Bosch was later acquitted and moved back to Miami while Posada would escape from prison, eventually moving back to the U.S. as well.

The U.S. Government could have easily prevented this horrible act of terrorism and were given all the information needed from an earlier incident in Jamaica: On July 9, 1976, Cuban terrorists tried to bomb the same plane. If that plane was not late, the bomb would have killed 29 passengers leaving from Jamaica to Havana.

U.S. Ambassador to Jamaica Sumner Gerard wrote in a cable that speculation on the bombers centered on Cuban exiles in Miami, and that the JLP was scared that the crime would be pinned on them after Manley linked caches of clandestine explosives to members of the JLP.

Two days after the bomb exploded in Jamaica, the offices of Trinidadian-owned British West Indian Airways was bombed in Barbados. The American ambassador speculated it was targeted because of its ties to Cuba and the fact that BWIA had recently established flights from Barbados to Angola. Bajan police also believed that the bombing might have been part of a U.S. destabilization effort.

On July 13, *The Daily Gleaner* carried an AP story that reported ORU (CORU) claimed responsibility for the blast and that Orlando Bosch was the head of the organization.[51] Ambassador Gerard wrote to Henry Kissinger to ask him that all information from U.S. agencies on the bombing be provided to the embassy and not the Jamaica government.

On July 23, Ambassador Gerard met with Michael Manley. After discussing the bombing incident in the airport, Gerard wrote to Kissinger:

> Given Manley's predisposition to believe we are behind all of his troubles and the keystone cop performance of his security forces when it comes to handling and evaluating intelligence, I believe we must be very careful and selective in passing information to the

---

51 US Embassy In Jamaica Cable (MIAMI TERRORISTS CLAIM BOMB BLAST) https://search.wikileaks.org/plusd/cables/1976KINGST02883_b.html

GOJ (Government Of Jamaica), lest we unnecessarily inflame an already nervous and paranoiac group.[52]

Gerard also met with Jamaican Security Minister Keble Munn and Superintendent Palmer of the Security Forces that same day. Palmer claimed he had an informant in Miami that gave him information on the location, which were the headquarters of Alpha 66. Gerard would write in a cable that the FBI had previously checked Alpha 66 to negative results, discarding the information he was given.

Gerard was obviously concerned with passing information on to Manley for one reason: the culprits for the bombing were mostly former or current CIA agents, the same people Manley was blaming for destabilizing the government. It is ironic that Gerard would blame Manley's Keystone Cops when the Jamaican police provided correct information on the culprits.

Alpha 66 was the anti-Castro terrorist groups that helped found CORU, the group that claimed responsibility for the bombing. CORU was headed by Antonio Veciana, the same man who worked for CIA agent David Atlee Phillips with Luis Posada to kill Castro in 1971. Veciana has admitted to working for the CIA between in 1961 and 1963 and claims that there was a CIA plot to kill President John F. Kennedy.

After a string of other bombings in Guyana, the Caribbean News Agency wrote an article that appeared in several West Indian newspapers with the headline, "Rebel Group May Step Up Terrorism In Carib." The article led off with:

A Miami based anti-Castro group that has claimed responsibility for recent bombings in some Caribbean

---

52 US Embassy In Jamaica Cable (MEETING WITH PRIME MINISTER MANLEY) https://search.wikileaks.org/plusd/cables/1976KINGST03115_b.html

countries, is likely to increase terrorist activities in the region, informed sources in Miami have said. The group, the United Revolutionary Organization (ORU) is having a congress in Miami this weekend to plan its future program of attacks on countries which are friendly to the revolutionary government of Cuba, the sources added. The Miami sources said that the group was formed recently of five counter-revolutionary organizations all based in Miami, and is understood to enjoy the tacit support of some branches of the United States intelligence services.[53]

The article further said that Orlando Bosch was the head of the terrorist group, and the Cuban terrorists said the bomb had been placed there because Guyana was friendly to the Cuban government, allowing Cuban troop transports bound for Angola to be refueled on Guyanese territory.

After the Guyanese consulate in Trinidad was bombed, Foreign Minister Frederick Wills contacted the American ambassador due to concerns that the Caribbean terrorism spree had been connected to U.S. intelligence agencies. Wills also expressed concern that he had heard reports of assassination plots for both the Guyanese and Jamaican Prime Ministers by Cuban exiles from respected journalist Gil Noble.

The American ambassador brought in the FBI legal attache in Venezuela, Joseph Leo, to address Wills concerns. Leo told Wills that the Cuban terrorists were not based in Miami and were, in fact, based in the Dominican Republic where the United States could not extradite them. Leo would also claim that the

---

53   US Embassy In Guyana Cable (GUYANESE CONCERN OVER CUBAN EXILE ACTIVITY) https://www.wikileaks.org/plusd/cables/1976GEORGE01777_b.html

U.S. government was in no way connected to or supported the Cuban terrorists.[54]

Joseph Leo was lying to the Foreign Minister; he knew very well the Cuban terrorists were not in the Dominican Republic but in Venezuela, where Leo was working at the embassy as a legal attache for the FBI. Leo was close with Posada and helped him obtain visas for friends and family members, despite the fact that Posada was known by the FBI to be an international terrorist and drug dealer.

A few weeks after Leo told the Guyanese foreign minister that the U.S. in no way supported the CORU terrorist organization, at the request of Luis Posada, Leo helped Hernan Ricardo Lozano get a visa to travel to Puerto Rico. Lozano told Leo that he was planning on attacking the Cuban Embassy and Leo was fully aware that Lozano worked for Posada. Also, Lozano's passport showed that he traveled to Trinidad on the date that the Guyanese consulate was bombed. Posada claimed in an interview that Leo and Lozano were friends.

Lozano, along with Freddy Lugo, was arrested in Trinidad hours after Cuban Flight 455 was blown up. The two immediately implicated Posada and Bosch as the organizers and funders of the plot. The phone number to FBI legal attache Joseph Leo was also found in the possession of Freddy Lugo.[55]

CIA documents show that in the September before the airline bombing, Orlando Bosch was in Venezuela with the knowledge and protection of Venezuelan President Carlos Perez. While in Venezuela, Bosch attended a dinner intended to raise money for

---

54 US Embassy In Guyana Cable (TERRORISM AND ASSASSINATION PLOTS: MEETING WITH WILLS)) https://search.wikileaks.org/plusd/cables/1976GEORGE01810_b.html

55 The National Security Archive, Bombing of Cuban Jetliner 30 Years Later (George Washinton University, 2006) http://nsarchive.gwu.edu/NSAEBB/NSAEBB202/

his terrorist cause. Along with Bosch, Posada, and FBI informant Ricardo Morales Navarrete, also claimed that Bosch would say, "Now that our organization has come out of the Letelier job looking good, it's time to move onto something else."[56]

The Letelier job Bosch was referring to was the assassination of former Chilean foreign minister and ambassador to the U.S. Orlando Letelier. Letelier would become a leading voice against the right-wing dictator Augusto Pinochet, who took control of Chile after a CIA-backed military coup in 1973. Letelier was living in Washington, D.C., where he was teaching at American University and working at the Transnational Institute.

On September 21, 1976, Letelier was driving down Embassy Row in Washington D.C. when his car blew up, killing him and his American assistant Ronni Moffitt and injuring her husband Michael.

Former CIA agent Michael Townley would be extradited from Chile to the United States and confessed to organizing the car bombing. Townley had worked for DINA, Pinochet's secret police who were infamous for their torture, assassinations, and general human rights violations. The head of DINA at the time was Manuel Contreras, who was also a paid CIA asset who would be convicted of the Letelier assassination in 1993 in Chile. Contreras claimed that the CIA sent Townley to Chile.

After consulting with Bosch and Posada, Townley wound up hiring five CORU associates of Bosch and Posada. They included Posada's close friend Dionisio Suarez Esquivel, Operation 40 veteran Alvin Ross Diaz, and brothers Guillermo and Ignacio Novo. Townley testified that it was Orlando Bosch and Luis

56   Ann Louise Bardach, Twilight Of The Assassins (The Atlantic,   2006)   http://www.theatlantic.com/magazine/archive/2006/11/twilight-of-the-assassins/305291/

Posada who collaborated with him on the plot and supplied the assassins to bomb Letelier.

The Novo brothers were no strangers to political assassinations, having been also implicated by CIA agent Marita Lorenz as being involved in the plot to kill Kennedy. Guillermo Novo was originally sentenced to life in prison, but both he and his brother got off on a technicality after a retrial. When Posada was arrested in Venezuela for plotting to blow up Cuban Flight 455, a map of Washington with Letelier's route to work was found in his possession.

Townley only served 52 months in jail for the murders of Letelier and Moffitt and later entered the witness protection program, despite being the mastermind of the plot. His Cuban cohorts were only given time served for their roles in the murders, being set free after originally being convicted and sentenced. Another man, Virgilio Paz Romero who was an Operation 40 member, was arrested in 1991 after 15 years in hiding and sentenced to 12 years in prison.

Despite the fact the FBI and CIA knew that Bosch and Posada were involved in the plot to kill Letelier, neither of them were charged with the crime. It is amazing to think that an act of terrorism that killed a professor and his aide, a female American citizen, went unpunished and was conducted in part by men closely connected to the CIA. The car bombing was not only an assassination but also an act of terrorism, in the heart of Washington D.C.'s international diplomatic center, Embassy Row.

Interestingly enough, Letelier's assassination wasn't the first time he was a target for the CIA and their Cuban underlings. In 1972, the infamous Watergate burglars would break into the Chilean Embassy, where Letelier was serving as ambassador.

The Letelier killing inspired the scene in *Scarface*, where Tony Montana is supposed to kill a man with a car bomb in New York City, according to Oliver Stone. The character Suarez from the movie was based on a real Bolivian cocaine kingpin of the same name, who was being protected by the CIA.

Despite the many connections of the Cuban terrorists of CORU to the CIA, many people might claim that their actions were of their own and they were acting as rogue agents. But the CIA actively protected those terrorists and when Posada broke out of prison, he was once again hired by George Bush to fund the Contras with drug money along with Felix Rodriguez during the Iran-Cocaine-Contra affair. Bush would also pardon Orlando Bosch, despite the fact that as head of the CIA in 1976 when Bosch planned the Letelier killing and the Cubana Flight 455 bombing, Bush knew about all of Bosch's terrorism.

If anything the CIA is guilty of creating a Frankenstein terrorist who has plagued Latin America and the Caribbean for four decades. Posada would tell *New York Times* reporter Louise Ann Bardache:

> The CIA taught us everything everything. They taught us explosives, how to kill, bomb, trained us in acts of sabotage. When the Cubans were working for the CIA they were called patriots. 'Acciones de sabotaje' acts of sabotage was the term they used to classify this type of operation, now they call it terrorism. The times have changed.[57]

"In Miami, I was on a CIA draw of $300 [a month] plus all expenses," Posada told reporter Blake Fleetwood. "Later the

---

57 James C. McKinley Jr., Terror Accusations, but Perjury Charges (The New York Times, 2011) http://www.nytimes.com/2011/01/10/us/10posada.html

CIA helped me set up my detective agency (in Venezuela) from which we planned actions."[58]

Posada would finally face U.S. authorities in 2005 when he was caught sneaking into the country on a false passport. In his defense, his lawyer would say:

> My client has been a soldier of the United States for 40 years, whether he is officially or unofficially today on the payroll, but the bottom line is my client is a product of this country. He was trained at Fort Benning in 1963. He has served in the Central Intelligence Agency. He was in El Salvador in the mid- 80s.[59]

Later in 2011, Posada faced charges for immigration fraud and perjury. His lawyer asked for certain CIA files to be declassified that showed the CIA ordered Posada to keep quiet, as well as all documents about Posada's work for the CIA until 1996, plus documentation regarding his work on behalf of the DISIP (the former Venezuelan intelligence service).

The documents were never declassified and Posada was found not guilty of his charges and is today a free man living in Miami, attending right-wing fundraisers.

While it is easy to write off Posada and his band of CIA trained narco-terrorists as rogue agents who acted outside the jurisdiction of the CIA, evidence shows that their actions were tolerated if not encouraged by the CIA. The U.S. Department of Justice had the chance to have the terrorist mastermind Orlando Bosch extradited from Venezuela and Costa Rica to face charges

---

58 Ann Louise Bardach, *Without Fidel: A Death Foretold in Miami, Havana and Washington* (Simon & Schuster, New York) 133.

59 Blake Fleetwood, Could Kissinger Have Prevented Letelier's Assassination 30 years Ago? (The Huffington Post, 2011) http://www.huffingtonpost.com/blake-fleetwood/could-kissinger-have-prev_b_29979.html

in the U.S. but declined to do so despite the fact that Bosch was allegedly plotting to assassinate Secretary of State Henry Kissinger.

Rather than punish Bosch for his crimes, it seems like the CIA would use Bosch's terrorism for their own advantage. Saul Landau, a friend and coworker of Orlando Letelier, wrote a book about his friend who was murdered by CORU. In that book he claimed that a Miami detective told him, "The Cubans held the CORU meeting at the request of the CIA. The Cuban groups... were running amok in the mid-1970s, and the United States had lost control of them. So the United States backed the meeting to get them all going in the same direction again, under United States control."

It is hard to believe that any of the CORU terrorists Orlando Bosch, Luis Posada, Frank Castro, and Guillermo Novo were not acting with the approval of the CIA. In the Letelier murder case, Novo's lawyer claimed that the CIA was behind the murder of Letelier. Both Posada and Castro would go on to be utilized by George H.W. Bush and the CIA during the Iran-Contra scandal.

The protection given to the CIA's secret team of Cuban narco-terrorists came back to haunt America after 9/11. When George W. Bush said, "We will make no distinction between the terrorists who committed these acts and those who harbor them," he neglected to bring up the terrorists the United States was harboring with the help of his father and his brother Jeb. The Bush family was closely tied to those terrorists dating back to Bush's involvement in Operation 40 as a CIA agent.

CHAPTER 13

THE BIN LADEN OF THE AMERICAS

1976 was not the first year that Jamaica was struck by terrorism. In 1974, the Cuban Embassy was bombed twice by a CIA-trained anti-Castro Cuban by the name of Orlando Bosch. Bosch was a pediatrician who had known Castro in college. As a member of the infamous Operation 40, Bosch was implicated by CIA agent Marita Lorenz as being involved in the plot to kill Kennedy along with E. Howard Hunt and Frank Sturgis.[60] After the Kennedy assassination, Bosch would go on to have a long and distinguished career in terrorism and extortion.

Bosch worked with the CIA directly in 1962 and in 1963, the year Kennedy was killed. In the years after JFK's assassination, Bosch went on an international terrorism spree that would last forty years. In 1968, Bosch was convicted of shooting a high-powered weapon at a Polish ship heading to Cuba and served four years in prison. According to the U.S. Department of Justice, Bosch was involved in more than 30 acts of terrorism; Cuban authorities put the number at more than 70. Bosch would also extort Cubans in Miami into giving him money to fund his terrorist campaigns.

---

60 Marita Lorenz, Frank Sturgis, Lee Harvey Oswald, Orlando Bosch (YouTube) https://www.youtube.com/watch?v=UhO21clPUXs

The death toll of Bosch's terrorism and assassinations would top more than a hundred. Despite his acts of terror and murder all over the world and in the U.S. as well, for his whole life, the American government would protect Bosch. One man in particular who would help him would be George H.W. Bush. As members of Operation 40, both Bush and Bosch would have worked together on anti-Castro operations. Bosch would reach his terrorist apex in 1976, when the U.S. Government chose not to extradite him from two different countries while George Bush was running the CIA.

Bosch's partner in crime and fellow terrorist, Luis Posada Carrilles, was a man just as devious with the same disregard for human life and hatred for Fidel Castro and those who were friendly with him. Unlike Bosch, Posada was also connected to the cocaine trade as well as the CIA. According to journalists Ernest Volkman and John Cummings Posada was seen at the sites of several explosions in Jamaica in 1976.[61]

Peter Kornbluh of the National Security Archive called Posada "one of the most dangerous terrorists in recent history and the godfather of Cuban exile violence. He is known in Cuba as the Osama Bin Laden of the Americas."

Like Bosch, Posada had known Fidel Castro from his days at the University of Havana. Posada had opposed Castro and his revolution from its start, which lead to him being detained in military prison before leaving for Mexico and the United States.

In the U.S., Posada would link up with the CIA and be involved in the planning of the Bay of Pigs Invasion. The CIA at Fort Benning in Georgia would train Posada in sabotage and explosives. He would later use that experience to train Cuban exiles for an invasion of Cuba.

---

61 Ernest Volkman and John Cummings, "Murder as Usual", Penthouse (New York), December 1977

Along with Bosch, he would also join the infamous Operation 40, the CIA assassination squad. Other members of the squad included notorious drug smuggler Barry Seal and Watergate criminals Bernard Barker, Frank Sturgis, and E. Howard Hunt.[62] Some of the other members of Operation 40, such as Felix Rodriguez, Ted Shackley, would play big roles in the Iran-Contra scandal. Several of the members of the group were tied to the Kennedy assassination, with E Howard Hunt admitting his involvement as well as that of fellow Operation 40 members, David Morales, Frank Sturgis, and David Atlee Phillips.

According to Fabian Escalante, the head of Cuban Intelligence, Operation 40 was organized by then-Vice President Richard Nixon who brought together a group of businessmen, including future President George H.W. Bush, to fund the group.

Presidents Nixon and Bush had close ties to members of Operation 40, and the members would be at the center of their biggest scandals, Watergate and Iran-Contra.

Like many of the men involved in Operation 40, Posada would be connected to the Kennedy assassination. Chauncey Holt, who claims to have worked both for the CIA as a document forger and for Miami gangster Meyer Lansky, claimed that Posada, along with fellow CORU founder Guillermo Novo, and Freddy Lugo, were involved in the JFK assassination.

In 1978, Posada was interviewed by the House Select Committee on Assassinations about the Kennedy assassination while in prison. Another associate of his, Antonio Veciana, was also interviewed by the HSCA. Veciana founded anti-Castro

---

62 Michael Carlson, Orlando Bosch: CIA-backed Cuban exile implicated in numerous anti-Castro terrorist operations, (The Independent, 2011) http://www.independent.co.uk/news/obituaries/orlando-bosch-cia-backed-cuban-exile-implicated-in-numerous-anti-castro-terrorist-operations-2304468.html

terrorist group, Alpha 66, that would plot along with Posada to kill Castro in 1971 and was convicted of conspiracy to distribute cocaine in 1974. Veciana claimed that he saw alleged JFK assassin Lee Harvey Oswald with his CIA handler, Maurice Bishop, in Dallas a few months before the assassination in 1963.

Later Veciana revealed that Maurice Bishop was David Atlee Phillips, the same man E Howard Hunt would implicate as being involved in the Kennedy assassination and claim that the Kennedy killing was planned by American military and intelligence officials.[63] In 1979, Veciana survived an assassination attempt when he was shot in the head. Several other people called to testify before the HSCA would not be so lucky.

Sam Giancana, the Chicago mob figure who has been implicated in the JFK assassination, was killed in an unsolved murder before being slated to testify to Congress about the Kennedy killing in 1975. Fellow mobster Johnny Roselli was also called to testify to Congress about the JFK murder, but was killed before he could do so, winding up with his body cut up in a drum in a Florida harbor.

Unlike the other men who were allegedly involved in the Kennedy assassination, Posada and Bosch did not talk about any CIA involvement in the plot and were rewarded with government protection and support and given a license to kill, deal drugs, and commit acts of terrorism.

Throughout Posada's whole career, he would be tied to two other men, both trained by the CIA to fight against Castro. One of these men, Felix Rodriguez, would go on to be a decorated CIA agent, fighting Communism in Latin America. Much of Rodriguez's work was done through assassinations and the drug trade. Another man, Jorge Mas Canosa, would go on to

---

63 Antonio Veciana, Admissions and Revelations (Vimeo) https://vimeo.com/121102412

be a powerful businessman and lobbyist who would use his government connections to fight against Castro.

All three men would stay friends after working for the Bay of Pigs and being trained by the CIA at Fort Benning. According to several sources, including Cuban intelligence head Fabian Escalante and researchers Paul Kangas and Dr. Carl Jensen, George H.W. Bush worked with Rodriguez to recruit Cuban exiles for the Bay of Pigs invasion, including Mas Canosa and Luis Posada.[64]

CIA documents show that Canosa was involved in Posada's international terrorism in the 60s. Posada claimed that Canosa continued funding his terrorist activities, including organizing his escape from a Venezuelan prison and financing his bombings, well into the 90s through his Cuban American National Foundation. According to Lt. Colonel Oliver North's notes,[65] Canosa was involved in funding Felix Rodriguez's missions during Iran-Contra. Posada would also work with Rodriguez in Iran-Contra, reuniting the three longtime friends in their covert war against Communism.

Canosa was also close with George H.W. Bush, the man many claim recruited him to work for the CIA. Bush would appoint Canosa chair of the President's Advisory Board for Cuba Broadcasting and fund his radio station for 25 million dollars a year. At a fundraiser, Bush saluted Jorge Mas Canosa as a living embodiment of the success of Cuban immigrants in the United States. Canosa was a big supporter of Bush and

---

64 Reinaldo Taladrid And Lazaro Baredo, The Bush family, the Cuban mafia and the Kennedy assassination (CMI Brasil, 2006) http://www.midi-aindependente.org/pt/blue/2006/01/342879.shtml

65 Mark J. Prendergast, Ex-agent Linked To Iran-contra Intrigue (Miami Sun Sentinel, 1988) http://articles.sun-sentinel.com/1988-07-24/news/8802120955_1_duane-dewey-clarridge-congress-iran-contra-felix-rodriguez

a powerful lobbyist connected to members of both political parties, including Bill Clinton.

Aside from his political and business connections, which also included Jeb Bush, Canosa also had a great deal of connections in the drug world. Canosa's Cuban American National Foundation would hire the Novo brothers, Guillermo and Ignacio.

Guillermo has been connected to everything from the JFK assassination to an attempted assassination of Che Guevara at the U.N. with a bazooka to the car-bombing murder of Chilean diplomat Orlando Letelier, as well as the cocaine trade and the terrorist organization CORU.

Canosa was also a big supporter of Orlando Bosch. After breaking Posada out of jail, Canosa was working behind the scenes to make sure Venezuela released his partner in crime as well. Canosa would testify at Bosch's parole hearing in Miami in 1988, calling him a friend for more than 20 years. It would be another old friend of Canosa's, George H.W. Bush, who would have Bosch released in 1990.

Posada broke out of prison in Venezuela in 1985 with the help of his old friends Jorge Mas Canosa and Felix Rodriguez. He returned to working with his long-time pal Felix Rodriguez in El Salvador, who was working with their old CIA recruiter, George H.W. Bush. Canosa would join his CIA agent and terrorist friend Rodriguez in El Salvador as a key political supporter of the Nicaraguan Contras fighting Communism.

Of the four close friends, George H.W. Bush was publicly close with two of them. Bush would have a great deal of communications and meetings with Rodriguez in the Iran-Contra 80s, while Jorge Mas Canosa, would raise money for his political campaigns and lobby his anti-Cuban agenda in Congress. While receiving money from the U.S. Government for his anti-Cuban propaganda radio station, Canosa funded the terrorist activities of Posada and Bosch. Posada later claimed that Bush was fully aware that he was working for Bush's Contra re-supply operation in El Salvador, being paid $3,000 a month plus expenses.

Posada, Rodriguez, and Mas Canosa would become the most successful and notorious of all the Cuban exiles trained by the CIA. All of them would receive the support from the American government and George H.W. Bush in particular. The terrorist acts of Posada and Bosch cannot be separated from Bush. Either he tolerated them or they were done on his direct orders.

Aside from his CIA connections, Posada also had serious connections with the American Mafia. A declassified CIA report lists several prominent mob figures, as being associates of Posada's, including Frank "Lefty" Rosenthal, Norman Rothman, and Herminio Diaz.[66]

Rosenthal was the inspiration for Sam Rothstein, the mob-connected gambling guru from the Martin Scorsese movie *Casino*. Before moving to Las Vegas to run several casinos for the Mafia, Rosenthal was based in Miami. Declassified CIA files show that Posada sold silencers and explosives that he had stolen from the CIA to Rosenthal right before Rosenthal was connected to several bombings in the Miami area. Rosenthal was aware that Posada was connected to the CIA and the CIA suspected that Posada was working for Rosenthal. FBI files show that Posada was very active in the arms trade and willing to sell to anyone, including right wing racist extremists from the Ku Klux Klan or the John Birch Society.

Another Posada associate was Norman Rothman, a Jewish gangster who worked closely with Mafia drug kingpin Santo Trafficante. Rothman operated the Sans Souci Casino in Havana

---

66 CIA File On Luis Posada Carilles (National Security Archive) http://nsarchive.gwu.edu/NSAEBB/NSAEBB202/HSCA00000346.pdf

before Castro's revolution. During his time in Cuba, Rothman would be charged with smuggling guns into the country, and the Treasury Department file on him claimed he was also importing cocaine to the U.S. from Cuba along with Trafficante. *The New York Times* also claimed that Rothman worked with Jack Ruby, the man who killed Lee Harvey Oswald, in his Cuban gun running operation.

Despite their close ties to Batista, Trafficante, and Rothman, like the smart gambling experts they were, they were also hedging their bets and helped arm Castro in case he was victorious in his revolution. Trafficante lost his bet and when Castro was victorious, he banished all the mobsters and shut down their casinos and put Trafficante in prison.

The New York Times also reported that Rothman was connected to Watergate burglar Frank Sturgis, who was helping to arm Castro as a CIA agent. They claim Sturgis was offered a large amount of money from the mob through Norman Rothman to have Sturgis kill Fidel Castro, Sturgis would turn down the offer but relay the information to the CIA, which would later use the Mafia in an assassination attempt on the Cuban leader.

Another of Posada's Mafia associates was Herminio Diaz. Diaz was Cosa Nostra drug kingpin Santo Trafficante's bodyguard and professional assassin. He was involved in the drug and gun trades as well. In 1966, Diaz infiltrated Cuba in a plot to kill Fidel Castro but wound up being killed by Cuban security forces. Another man with Diaz, Tony Cuesta, was captured and later told Cuban Counterintelligence head Fabian Escalante that Diaz had told him the he was the gunman who had killed Kennedy in Dallas.[67]

---

67 Lamar Waldron, Thom Hartmann, *Legacy of Secrecy: The Long Shadow of the JFK Assassination* (Counterpoint, New York) 342.

According to CIA declassified reports, Posada was involved in international gun running in the Bahamas and the overthrow of the Guatemalan government, as well as making bombs for anti-Castro terrorists all while reporting to the CIA and being paid $400 a month.

In 1968, the CIA relocated Posada to Venezuela because of his ties to organized crime in Miami and his relationship with Frank "Lefty" Rosenthal and others and because he was stealing explosives and other CIA property. At this time, the Venezuelan government was battling leftist guerillas and had banned opposing political parties. Posada worked his way into becoming the head of their version of the CIA, the DISIP, while still working for the CIA.

In 1970, Posada was investigated for selling weapons stolen from an Army base in South Carolina to insurgents in Guyana. The investigation headed by the FBI report lists Posada as a gangster type who would kill pro-Castro types before questioning them.

The CIA had given several Cuban former agents a license to kill, commit acts of terrorism, deal drugs and weapons, and to launder money. Perhaps many of the CIA-trained Cubans were able to avoid prosecution by the law due to their knowledge of CIA secrets, including their involvement in the JFK assassination and government-sanctioned drug dealing. It could also be that all the terrorism, assassinations, and drug dealing done by the CIA-trained Cubans were done on the direct orders of the CIA and its secret team headed by Bush.

Posada would go on to a long and distinguished career in terrorism that spanned five decades. In 1990, Posada was shot in Guatemala City. While recuperating in Honduras, the FBI would suspect him of orchestrating 40 bombings in that country.

In 1997, Posada would be responsible for terrorist bombing of Cuban tourist locations that killed an Italian tourist.

In 2000, Posada was arrested in Panama with 33 pounds of explosives and convicted of plotting to assassinate his old enemy Fidel Castro at a meeting of Latin American leaders along with fellow narco-terrorist-assassin, Guillermo Novo. In 2004, Panamanian President Mireya Moscoso, a close ally of the Bush administration, pardoned Posada. Posada returned to the U.S. and was charged with immigration fraud in 2005, only to be set free by another Bush administration ally, Judge Kathleen Cardone.

In 2013, the Venezuelan government claimed that Luis Posada sent 400 mercenaries through Colombia on a mission to kill President Nicolas Maduro. At age 85, 50 years after he was involved in the conspiracy to kill Kennedy, Posada was once again involved in a murder conspiracy of a president. With the training, funding, and protection of the U.S. Government, the CIA, and in particular George H.W. Bush and his two sons, Posada has had 50 years of terrorism, drug dealing, illegal weapons, and assassinations.[68]

In Cuba, the place that Posada has terrorized for years, he is known as the Bin Laden of the Americas. By his own son's logic, George H.W. Bush was as guilty as the terrorists he harbored. The Bush family while publicly waging a war on drugs, privately facilitated the sales of hundreds of tons of cocaine.

---

68 Tim Elfrink, LUIS POSADA CARILLES LED 400 MEN TO ASSAS-SINATE VENEZUELA'S PRESIDENT, CARACAS SAYS (The Miami New Times, 2013) http://www.miaminewtimes.com/news/luis-posada-carilles-led-400-men-to-assassinate-venezuelas-president-caracas-says-6529737

CHAPTER 14

THE CIA'S CUBAN MAFIA

One month before the attempted bombing of the Cuban airplane leaving from Jamaica in June of 1976, the leaders of five anti-Castro Cuban groups had a meeting in the Dominican Republic. Among these groups were the AC (Accion Cuba) headed by Orlando Bosch, the FLNC (the National Liberation Front Of Cuba), which was headed by Frank Castro, as well as the MNC, which included members such as Guillermo Novo. Also included was Brigade 2506, Cuban exile veterans of the failed Bay Of Pigs invasion of Cuba, and a splinter group from that Brigade, the Movimento De 17 Abril (Movement of April 17, the date of the failed Bay of Pigs invasion).

Besides the fact that they all hated Castro, these groups had two other things in common: CIA training and the trafficking of cocaine. Frank Castro participated in the Bay of Pigs invasion and later received CIA training at Fort Jackson. Numerous CIA reports connect Frank Castro to the international cocaine trade, and he was arrested in part of an investigation of a Miami-based cocaine ring who was importing cocaine with the help of the Bolivian military dictatorship, but was only convicted of weapons possession after a key witness was murdered.

Castro would tell the Miami Herald that he started CORU because "I believe that the United States has betrayed freedom fighters around the world. They trained us to fight, brainwashed us how to fight, and now they put Cuban exiles in jail for what they had been taught to do in the early years."[69]

Frank Castro, along with several other Cuban Operation 40 veterans like Luis Posada and Felix Rodriguez, were later involved in the Iran-Contra cocaine scandal. Government documents show Castro was suspected of moving cocaine with Contra leader Eden Pastora in Costa Rica and was known as the liaison between the Medellin Cocaine Cartel, the Contras, and the anti-Castro Cubans during the 1980s.[70] Documents also show that Castro was involved in a plot by Colombian drug traffickers including Pablo Escobar, to kill U.S. Ambassador Lewis Tambs in Costa Rica.

When Senator John Kerry investigated the Iran-Contra cocaine connections, the Reagan/Bush administration would withhold information dealing with Castro's cocaine connections, stonewalling his investigation.

There are several reasons many of the CIA-trained Cubans went on to become involved in the cocaine trade. Santo Trafficante, who was running a narcotics trafficking operation in Cuba before Castro took over, recruited many of the Operation 40 and Brigade 2506 members. Many of the Cubans recruited were already involved in organized crime and drug dealing before becoming involved with the CIA.

The CIA offered great training to the Mafia Cubans that would allow them to later take control of the drug trade in Miami. The Cubans were trained by the American government to smuggle weapons into Cuba, in assassinations and guerilla warfare, and

69 Jonathan Marshall, Peter Dale Scott, Jane Hunter, *The Iran-Contra Connection: Secret Teams and Covert Operations in the Reagan Era* (South End Press, Boston 1987) 342

70 Peter Dale Scott And Jonathan Marshall, *Cocaine Politics: Drugs, Armies, and the CIA in Central America, Updated Edition* (University of California Press, 1988) 134.

then sent all over Latin America to fight Communism. Frank Castro would build connections in Bolivia; Guillermo Novo would work with the infamous Chilean Secret police; DINA and Luis Posada would run the Venezuelan secret police DISIP.

The training and access given by the CIA allowed this group to take over the cocaine trade from Latin America into the United States. The CIA also gave this group the home base of Miami, which due to its location, is an ideal entry point for cocaine from Latin America. Like James Bond and the fictional spies in TV and the movies, the CIA Cuban agents were above the law, and were subsequently protected by the American government. The CIA would not simply look the other way at the anti-Castro Cuban drug dealing, but they would use it to their advantage in covertly funding illegal wars.

Guillermo Novo was another veteran of the Bay of Pigs who served under alleged JFK assassin Frank Sturgis in Operation 40. According to Sturgis:

> This assassination group (Operation 40) would, upon orders, assassinate either members of the military or the political parties of the foreign country that you were going to infiltrate, and if necessary some of your own members who were suspected of being foreign agents... We were concentrating strictly in Cuba at that particular time.[71]

In 1964, Novo tried to shoot a bazooka at the United Nations when Che Guevara was speaking. Like the others, Novo would be linked to the international drug trade. When he was arrested

---

71 Dick Russell, *The Man Who Knew Too Much* (Carrol & Graf, 2003) 330.

in 1978, he was with Alvin Ross who had a large bag of cocaine and Manuel Menendez, an infamous Mexican heroin kingpin.[72]

Another man who provided a great deal of the financing for CORU was another veteran from the Bay of Pigs, Guillermo Hernandez Cartaya who headed the World Finance Corporation. The WFC was widely known for laundering money from drug and arms trafficking.[73] In fact, in the 1970s, the WFC was known as the largest and longest running money laundering agencies for Colombian cocaine smugglers.

Despite the fact that the WFC was investigated for laundering money from drugs and arms trafficking by the IRS, the DEA, and the FBI, the CIA, who objected to the Justice Department because several people being investigated were of interest to them, derailed the investigation. FBI files showed that several people suspected of being tied to terrorism were employed by the WFC.

The WFC was also closely tied to Santo Trafficante and his drug organization,[74] as were several Cuban-American narcotics traffickers, Colombian drug cartels, and CIA agents. Cartaya ran the monetary wing of the Cuban narco-terrorists. Providing them with funds and laundering their drug money. Cartaya, like many anti-Castro Cubans, had ties to the Bush family and was a close business associate of George H.W. Bush's son Jeb Bush. Jeb Bush would use his father's connections to the CIA-trained Cuban drug lords, money launderers, and terrorists to

---

72 Peter Dale Scott And Jonathan Marshall, *Cocaine Politics: Drugs, Armies, and the CIA in Central America*, Updated Edition (University of California Press, 1988) 33.

73 Peter Dale Scott And Jonathan Marshall, *Cocaine Politics: Drugs, Armies, and the CIA in Central America*, Updated Edition (University of California Press, 1988) 93.

74 Dan E. Moldea, *Interference: How Organized Crime Influences Professional Football* (William Morrow & Co, 1989)

gain power in Florida. Like many of his Cuban cohorts, Cartaya was involved in the Iran-Contra scandal, using his financial knowledge and know-how to launder money to the Contras.

CORU, consisting of CIA-trained members of Brigade 2506, and several other anti-Castro groups were more than an ideologically driven terrorist group. As narco-terrorists, they not only used drugs to finance their terrorism, but they used terrorism to expand their drug empire.

The terrorism in Jamaica was not only sent as a message to stay away from Castro but also to intimidate the Jamaican government into allowing the narcotics trade to flow freely from their country, just as the Colombian and Mexican drug cartels have used terrorism to intimidate governments into allowing drugs to flow freely from their countries.

CHAPTER 15

A BRIEF HISTORY OF THE CENTRAL INTELLIGENCE AGENCY

The Central Intelligence Agency is one of the most despicable organizations of all time, killing, lying, and dealing drugs, all in the name of America. It was founded in 1946 after the defeat of Nazi Germany and was used to secretly fight the new evil of Communism. In doing so, the CIA has acted with little oversight when they believed the ends justified the means even if the means include large-scale narcotics trafficking, terrorism, and even the assassination of an American president.

In the CIA's fight against Communism, Fidel Castro has been the Road Runner to their Wile E. Coyote. No matter what they try to do to kill him, it never works out. From the failed Bay of Pigs invasion to using women to poison him to terrorism to exploding cigars, they could never get him. Any friend of Castro's was an enemy of the CIA, as Jamaican Prime Minister Michael Manley would learn.

For the CIA, the Bay of Pigs was their 9/11, a great tragedy to be remembered and used as a rallying point. Feeling betrayed by American President John F. Kennedy for not supporting them in the Bay of Pigs operation, the CIA and the forces behind them turned their target from Castro to Kennedy. Several former CIA agents, government officials, Cuban Intelligence agents, historians, and journalists have all made the claim that the CIA was behind the assassination of JFK.

Still, assassinations and drug dealing are only a small part of the CIA's strategy; propaganda and economic sabotage are more typically what the CIA engages in under the name of capitalism and the American way and to destroy governments they believe are enemies.

Outside of Cuba, the CIA also attempted to kill progressive African President Patrice Lumumba in what was then Zaire; supported the murderous dictator Mobutu Sese Seko; and used its own airline, Air America, to import heroin from Laos to the U.S. Many CIA agents or assets are big players in the drug trade, like Manuel Noriega or terrorist masterminds like Luis Posada Carrilles.

In many ways, the CIA has acted as the international organized crime element of the American government. Its actions of narco-trafficking, arms dealing, and assassinations are quite similar to that of the Mafia. Like the Mafia, its secrecy and government contacts allow them to avoid government persecution for their illegal activities.

There are several reasons the CIA became involved in narco-trafficking. Illegal money from narcotics is a convenient and discreet way to fund armies without a paper trail. Drug dealers also tend to be discreet about their activities and are not likely to go to law enforcement or the media. In many third-world countries, the drug trade is one of the biggest sources of income, so the people who control the drug trade often control the country. In Nicaragua, the CIA not only illegally funded the pro-American Contras, but also played a big part in the drug dealing that was used to fund them as well. Wherever the CIA goes, so goes a pattern of propaganda, gun running, drug dealing, assassinations, military coups and governments that often wind up with corrupt murderous dictators who still get support from their CIA benefactors. All this happens in the name of capitalism.

Amazingly within the CIA, one of the most clandestine organizations on Earth, there exists a smaller, even more secret team whose actions are unknown to all except a select few within the CIA; a group of individuals bent on capitalist domination of the United States and the world. This team was born out of the Bay of Pigs invasion and included politicians such as Prescott Bush; CIA agents such as his son, George H.W. Bush; Ted Shackley, E. Howard Hunt, Frank Sturgis, and the Cubans who worked for them: Felix Rodriguez, Luis Posada Carilles, and Orlando Bosch.

It is believed by many that this team was involved in the Kennedy assassination, Watergate scandal, and the attempted cover-ups of both. Ted Shackley would bring some of the anti-Castro Cubans, such as the infamous Felix Rodriguez, with him to Laos during the Vietnam War, where they would operate heroin smuggling operations to fund the anti-Communist forces of General Vang Pao, with long-time CIA asset and mob boss Santo Trafficante.[75]

In 1976, George H.W. Bush became Director of the CIA. Shortly after, the Cuban faction of the secret team would go on an assassination and terrorism spree. As Vice President during the 1980s, Bush reunited with members of that same secret team during the Iran-Contra affair to use the cocaine trade to fund the Nicaraguan Contras.

---

75 Alfred W. McCoy, *The Politics of Heroin: CIA Complicity in the Global Drug Trade* (Chicago Review Press, 2003)

Bush's second-in-command, Ted Shackley, was another secret team member with connections to the narco-terrorist Cuban wing of the CIA from the Bay of Pigs fiasco. He was well versed in using the narcotics trade to fund anti-Communist forces from his days in Laos. Shackley was also a master plotter of assassinations, tactics he used both against Cuba in Operation 40 and in Laos, and was according to several sources running a top-secret assassination program that involved Felix Rodriguez, Luis Posada Carilles, and Rafael "Chi Chi" Quintero.

The patterns and behavior of the CIA and the secret team are very important in understanding what the CIA was doing in Jamaica in 1976. Both George H.W. Bush and Ted Shackley were part of a group of individuals who conspired to work with domestic and foreign organized crime groups in the trafficking of arms and narcotics, and that would plot coups and assassinations, both domestically and internationally.

Along with Shackley and Bush and their secret team came the many CIA-trained anti-Castro Cubans who would do their dirty work. These Cubans included narco-terrorist Luis Posada Carrilles, the man who killed Che Guevara, and George H.W. Bush's good friend Felix Rodriguez, terrorist mastermind Orlando Bosch, and several others involved in the JFK assassination, Watergate, and Iran-Contra affairs.

CHAPTER 16

THE FAMILY JEWELS, WATERGATE, AND JFK

Before the CIA began major operations in Jamaica in 1976, it dealt with a scandal that almost revealed some of its darkest secrets, including a possible involvement in the JFK assassination. The Watergate scandal that ended Richard Nixon's career would begin when two CIA veterans, E. Howard Hunt and Frank Sturgis, were implicated in bugging the Democratic National Committee headquarters on June 17, 1972, at the Watergate Hotel.

Among the five burglars caught at the Watergate Hotel were two anti-Castro Cubans who had worked for the CIA, Virgilio Gonzalez and Eugenio Martinez. Frank Sturgis later admitted to planning to kill Castro at the behest of the CIA and was also believed to be involved in the Bay of Pigs failure. Frank McCord, another CIA employee, was also arrested. These men led investigators to E. Howard Hunt, who had organized the burglary and bugging.

Hunt was a long-time CIA agent who organized the overthrow of the democratically elected president in Guatemala in 1954, and would later be the point person in Cuba, organizing anti-Castro Cubans in their opposition to Castro and helping plan the Bay of Pigs invasion. He also worked as the assistant to CIA head Allen Dulles and helped him write a book. Hunt retired from the CIA in 1970, only to work for a CIA front company, the Robert R. Mullen Company, and later for Nixon in the President's Special Investigations Unit.

Richard Nixon rightfully feared that the Watergate incident could blow up into a bigger scandal than a simple burglary and become a major scandal for the CIA. He was caught on tape telling his Chief of Staff, H.R. Haldeman:

> Very bad, to have this fellow Hunt, ah, you know, ah, it's, he, he knows too damn much and he was involved, we happen to know that. And that it gets out that the whole, this is all involved in the Cuban thing, that it's a fiasco, and it's going to make the FBI, ah CIA look bad, it's going to make Hunt look bad, and it's likely to blow the whole, uh, Bay of Pigs thing which we think would be very unfortunate for CIA and for the country at this time, and for American foreign policy, and he just better tough it and lay it on them.[76] You open that scab and there's a hell of a lot of things, and we just feel that it would be very detrimental to have things go any further. This involves these Cubans, Hunt and a lot of hanky-panky that we have nothing to do with ourselves.

Later in his book *The Ends of Power*, Haldeman admitted that Nixon was referring to the Kennedy assassination when he spoke about "the whole Bay of Pigs thing."[77] One could surmise

---

76 Transcript Of Nixon's Meeting With H.R. Haldeman, June 23rd 1972 http://nixon.archives.gov/forresearchers/find/tapes/watergate/trial/exhibit_02.pdf

77 Stephen J. Revele And Christopher Wilkinson, Critic's Ploy to Review 'Nixon' Is the Only Dirty Trick (The L.A. Times 1996) http://articles.latimes.

that the hanky-panky could be the Kennedy assassination, and the Cubans Nixon was referring to could be those from the CIA-sponsored Operation 40, also implicated in the assassination.

Hunt served 33 months in prison for his involvement in the Watergate burglary and would later be pardoned by President Gerald Ford, but Nixon's fear of the Bay of Pigs thing blowing up and making the CIA look bad never happened.

In a recorded deathbed confession, E. Howard Hunt would admit to his role in the JFK killing and implicate President Lyndon B. Johnson, CIA agents David Atlee Phillips, Cord Meyer, William Harvey, Frank Sturgis, as well as anti-Castro Cuban, Antonio Veciana. His confession reads:

> Cord Meyer discusses a plot with [David Atlee] Phillips who brings in Wm. Harvey and Antonio Veciana. He meets with Oswald in Mexico City. . . . Then Veciana meets w/ Frank Sturgis in Miami and enlists David Morales in anticipation of killing JFK there. But LBJ changes itinerary to Dallas, citing personal reasons.[78]

It was alleged that Cord Meyer's ex-wife was having an affair with JFK. Meyer's wife later died in an unsolved crime and some close to Meyer believed the CIA did it.

William King Harvey was a CIA agent in charge of the assassinations of foreign leaders, including Castro. Harvey also utilized the American Mafia, including Chicago gangsters Sam Giancana, Santo Trafficante, Jr., and Johnny Roselli in attempts to kill Castro. Former mob associates also implicated Roselli in the plot to kill JFK. Sam Giancana allegedly helped JFK get

---

com/1996-01-01/entertainment/ca-19897_1_richard-nixon

78 Erik Hedegaard, The Last Confession Of E. Howard Hunt (Rolling Stone 2007) http://www.rollingstone.com/culture/features/the-last-confession-of-e-howard-hunt-20070405

elected at the behest of his father, Joseph Kennedy. Both his nephew[79] and his lawyer[80] claimed that Giancana was involved in the plot to kill Kennedy after Kennedy repaid Giancana's election favor by having his brother Robert Kennedy put pressure on his mob activities and also had an affair with his mistress. Before Jack Ruby killed Lee Harvey Oswald, he met with Trafficante and another mob associate.

Gaeton Fonzi, the staff investigator of the House Select Committee on Assassinations, would write in his book *The Last Investigation*, that he believed both Antonio Veciana and William Harvey were involved in the murder of JFK[81]. Veciana was an anti-Castro Cuban who had plotted to kill Fidel Castro with a bazooka on the order of David Atlee Phillips. Veciana also founded Alpha 66, an anti-Castro group that received a great deal of funding from the CIA. After the Cuban Missile Crisis, Veciana angered Kennedy when Alpha 66 attacked a Soviet ship in the Cuban harbor and later held a press conference claiming that the attack had U.S. support. Kennedy ordered that Veciana be arrested along with other members of Alpha 66. Veciana, along with several other anti-Castro Cubans, would wind up in the drug trade and he was ultimately sentenced to seven years in New York City for conspiring to distribute cocaine. Antonio Veciana recently admitted that there was a CIA conspiracy to kill Kennedy that involved David Atlee Phillips[82].

79 Sam Giancana and Chuck Giancana, *Double Cross: The Story of the Man Who Controlled America* (Little, Brown, 1992)

80 Frank Ragano And Selwyn Raab, *Mob Lawyer* (Prentice Hall & IBD, 1994)

81 Gaeton Fonzi, *The Last Investigation* (The Mary Ferrell Foundation, 1994)

82 Antonio Veciana - Admissions and Revelations, (Vimeo) https://vimeo.com/121102412

Hunt's old pal and cohort in the Watergate burglary, Sturgis, also was involved in anti-Castro activities in Cuba. Sturgis attempted to have Castro killed by using a former lover of his, Marita Lorenz, to poison him. Lorenz later claimed that Sturgis was involved in the Kennedy assassination and that he conspired with terrorists Orlando Bosch and Guillermo Novo to plot the killing with a group known as Operation 40. Operation 40 was started by Richard Nixon and George H.W. Bush. Many members of Operation 40 would achieve infamy through drug dealing, like Barry Seal, and terrorism, like Bosch and Posada Carilles, while others, including Felix Rodriguez, would play a big part in the Iran-Contra scandal.

The CIA managed to keep the Kennedy assassination under wraps even after several of its plotters were arrested for the Watergate burglary. Rather than disclosing its involvement in the murder of an American President, the CIA disclosed other dirt they did in a document known as the Family Jewels. This report was released to members of Congress but was not accessible to the general public until 2007.

But in 1973, under pressure from the press due to the involvement of CIA agents in the Watergate burglary, the CIA did release some of its deepest darkest secrets. Some of these secrets included conspiring with the Mafia figures Sam Giancana and Johnny Roselli to kill Castro, spying on anti-war activists and journalists in the U.S., and experimenting on humans with drugs such as LSD without their knowledge[83]. The CIA's image was dealt a blow by the release of these dark secrets, and the majority of Americans would never see the agency in the same light again. To say that there was any actual effect on the CIA's ability to operate independently is another thing.

---

83 The CIA Family Jewels (FOIA Document) http://www.foia.cia.gov/collection/family-jewels

The CIA's admitted connections to Trafficante are very telling. Trafficante, above all Mafia figures, was key in the international importation of cocaine and heroin into the United States. Trafficante, along with mobster Meyer Lansky, not only ran a casino in Cuba but used Cuba as a base for narcotics trafficking. Many of the Cubans recruited by the CIA were part of Trafficante's crime organization and already were involved in narcotics.

Trafficante was based out of Florida and was closely connected to Cuba before Castro's revolution. Before the Castro takeover, Trafficante had control over a good deal of the casino gambling and narcotics trade in Cuba. Trafficante earned the loyalty of many Cubans in his illegal activities and would offer his Cuban thugs to the CIA in their war against Castro.

It would seem as if Trafficante was the Mafia representative in the CIA secret team and a connection in both the narcotics trade and the Mafia. Trafficante continued his association with the CIA long after the Kennedy assassination. During the Vietnam War, Trafficante again teamed up with CIA agent Ted Shackley. In Laos, Shackley arranged a meeting with heroin kingpin and Laotian General Vang Pao and Trafficante.

One of the Watergate burglars, Bernard Barker, was also closely tied to Trafficante and his criminal organization. In fact, according to lawyer Daniel Sheehan, many members of the infamous Operation 40 assassination squad, were also members of Trafficante's Cuban Mafia. Frank Sturgis also worked closely with Trafficante in anti-Castro efforts.

The CIA's involvement with Trafficante explains a lot of the drug trafficking and organized crime connections the agency has maintained. The anti-Castro Cuban terrorists were part of the union between Trafficante and the CIA. Trained in espionage, torture, sabotage, assassinations, and other dirty tricks by the

CIA, with a background in organized crime and drug trafficking, a new Cuban Mafia would blur the line between organized crime and the CIA.

When Castro took over Cuba, Trafficante and his Mafia connections lost a major shipment point for narcotics. Jamaica, along with several countries, would soon replace Cuba as drug hubs for cocaine, heroin, and marijuana bound for America. Member of the CIA-sponsored Cuban Mafia would become key figures in the international drug trade from South America through the Caribbean and Central America and into the United States.

Unlike his fellow Mafia figures Johnny Roselli and Sam Giancana, who conspired with the CIA and were both killed in unsolved murders, Trafficante died a peaceful death in 1987, shortly after being implicated in the Iran-Contra affair.

As a member of the secret team and keeper of the secrets behind Kennedy's assassination, Trafficante seemed to have immunity against federal prosecution and Mafia killings. As did his army of anti-Castro Cubans, who would become the goons of the secret team, conducting their dirty work. While some of these Cubans may have left the employment of the CIA, they never left the secret team and would continue to conspire with the CIA, which is evident in 1976 Jamaica.

George H.W. Bush was also a member of the Secret Team and collaborated with these same Cuban Mafia that was born from Trafficante's partnership with the CIA. Under George H.W. Bush, the Secret Team would once again be in firm control of the CIA. Jamaica would be one of the first efforts Bush would take on as Director in 1976.

The history of the CIA and its Secret Team is important to understanding its involvement in Jamaica. Taking a James

Bond License to Kill approach, the CIA had become a mob-like organization with no sense of morality.

For the CIA, the ends of fighting Communism justified the means, including their documented use of torture, propaganda, forgery, burglary, kidnapping, military coups, civil wars, and lying. Jamaica was just one out of dozens of countries that felt the wrath of the CIA. By befriending Castro, Manley made himself a target in the secret war by the Secret Team that was controlling the CIA.

Manley warned of a Mafia attempt to take over Jamaica that was tied to a destabilization program before calling a State of Emergency. Journalists Ernest Volkman and John Cummings claim the CIA's small army of anti-Castro Cubans played a key role in the CIA's secret war in Jamaica. Given the history of the CIA's Secret Team in the Bay of Pigs, JFK assassination, Laos, Watergate and later Iran-Contra, allegations of narco-trafficking, assassination plots, and the fueling of violence must be taken seriously.

CHAPTER 17

THE SECRET HISTORY OF THE BUSH FAMILY

During 1976, when the CIA was actively trying to destabilize Jamaica, its director was George H.W. Bush, who later became Vice President and then President of the United States. During his hearings to become Director of the CIA, Bush testified that he had no previous ties to the CIA before 1975, but there is significant evidence that would say otherwise.

According to memos, Bush had been involved with the CIA since 1963. Bush served in the Navy at the age of 18 in 1942 and continued there until the end of World War II in 1945. After the war, he followed in his father's footsteps and attended Yale University and joined the university's secret society, Skull and Bones.

By the time Bush graduated from Yale, it had become a breeding ground for the CIA. Many Yale students had previously joined the predecessor to the CIA, the OSS, which conducted intelligence for the Navy. In the Yale class of 1943, there were a total of 35 students who went on to the CIA, according to Yale graduate, Skull And Bones member, and CIA agent Osborne Day.

Other Yale and Skull and Bones alumni who would work for the CIA included William Sloane Coffin, a classmate of Bush's from Phillips Academy. Bush brought Coffin into Skull and Bones, and later, Coffin would go on to work as a case officer for the CIA in West Germany. The CIA's dubious activities in Guatemala and Iran led to Coffin leaving the CIA and becoming an anti-war and civil rights activist.

Another Yale and Skull and Bones alumni who worked for the CIA was Richard Drain, class of 1943. Drain was one of the masterminds of the CIA's failed Bay of Pigs Invasion. Other Yale and Skull and Bones alumni connected to the Bay of Pigs include McGeorge Bundy, who graduated Yale in 1940, and his brother William Bundy.

William Bundy graduated Yale in 1939 and went to work for the Army in World War II working to crack Nazi codes. Bundy returned from the war and entered Harvard Law School before joining the CIA in the 50s as the chief of staff for the Office of National Estimates. He was very influential in the escalation of the Vietnam War while working in the Eisenhower, Kennedy, and Johnson administrations.

McGeorge Bundy, William's brother, became an Intelligence Officer for the Army in WWII and later worked for the Council On Foreign Relations, working closely with Allen Dulles, Director of the CIA, and Richard Bissell, a fellow Yale graduate who also worked for the CIA on covert operations in Europe. Bissell was Dulles' CIA Deputy Director of Plans who would oversee the CIA black operations, including plans to overthrow the governments of Guatemala, The Congo, Iran, and the Dominican Republic as well as the failed Bay of Pigs invasion.

McGeorge worked for both the JFK and LBJ administrations as National Security Advisor, where he played a major role in the Bay of Pigs and the Cuban missile crisis. Five days after the Kennedy assassination, McGeorge sent a memo, NSAM 273, encouraging escalation in the Vietnam War. Later research has proven that the memo was drafted a day before Kennedy was killed, yet the memo remained the same, leading many to believe that McGeorge had previous knowledge of the JFK assassination plot.[84]

Yet another Yale Skull and Bonesman was James Jesus Angleton, class of 1941. Norman Holmes Pearson, Yale's director of American Studies to the OSS, recruited Angleton, like he did with many Yale-bred CIA agents. Angleton received training by the British covert agency MI6 before becoming one of the first CIA agents during its founding year of 1947.

Angleton became the CIA liaison to the Israeli secret agency the Mossad before going on to be the Counter Intelligence Chief from 1954 to 1975. After the Kennedy assassination, he was in charge of investigating the agency's involvement with Lee Harvey Oswald and was accused of stonewalling the investigation by withholding information.

Aside from covering up the CIA's relationship with Oswald, Angleton would also be involved in another way to stop the investigation into JFK's murder. Before his death, John F. Kennedy was sleeping with CIA agent Cord Meyer's ex-wife, Mary Pinchot Meyer. Years later, in 1976, Angleton was caught breaking into Mary Meyer's house to steal her diary, which detailed information on her affair with JFK and her belief that the CIA was behind his assassination. Cord Meyer was a close friend of Angleton's, yet another Yale graduate who was part of another secret society at Yale, the Scroll and Key club.

---

84 James K. Galbraith, Exit Strategy: In 1963, JFK ordered a complete withdrawal from Vietnam (The Boston Review, 2003) http://bostonreview. net/us/galbraith-exit-strategy-vietnam

Meyer was named by E. Howard Hunt as one of the people behind the JFK assassination. Mary would be killed a year after Kennedy was killed in an unsolved murder. Peter Janney, the son of CIA director of personnel, Wistar Janney and close friend of the Meyer family would claim that the CIA killed Mary and that his father was part of the conspiracy to murder her. According to Janney, Walter Mitchell, who testified in Mary Meyer's murder trial confessed to killing her on behalf of the CIA.[85]

According to Janney, Mary was going to go public to dispute the Warren Commission right before she was murdered. Cord Meyer, who ran the CIA propaganda and press misinformation program Operation Mockingbird, also tried to obstruct the investigation into the CIA's role in Watergate.

Aside from George H.W. Bush's connections to the CIA through Yale and Skull and Bones, he also was tied to the agency through his family. Bush's father Prescott was a good friend with Allen Dulles. Dulles was a member of the OSS who would go on to run the CIA from 1952 until 1961.

As CIA chief, Dulles would oversee and plan the 1953 coup that overthrew the government of Iran and the 1954 coup that overthrew the government of Guatemala. Dulles also established the infamous Operation 40 and their act of government-sponsored terrorism when the group blew up a Belgian ship in the Havana harbor, killing 75 people and injuring 200. Dulles also helped hatch the assassination plot against Castro using Mafia figures Sam Giancana, Johnny Roselli, Santo Trafficante, Meyer Lansky, and Carlos Marcello, many of the same mob figures implicated in the JFK assassination.

---

85 Peter Janney, Mary's Mosaic: *The CIA Conspiracy to Murder John F. Kennedy, Mary Pinchot Meyer, and Their Vision for World Peace* (Skyhorse Publishing, 2013)

Dulles was an integral part of the Bay of Pigs invasion. After its failure, Kennedy said he would splinter the CIA into a thousand pieces and scatter it into the winds. Kennedy fired Dulles and his Skull and Bones deputy director Richard Bissell, angering the many CIA agents and other people loyal to Dulles. In 2015, Salon founder David Talbot released the book *The Devil's Chessboard: Allen Dulles, the CIA, and the Rise of America's Secret Government,* that claims Allen Dulles effectively ordered the hit on John Kennedy[86].

One of the people Kennedy angered was Prescott Bush, George H.W. Bush's father. Prescott would recommend people for Dulles to employ in the CIA. The then-Senator from Connecticut, Bush, defended Dulles in the Senate and praise the CIA as a defender of national security after the Bay of Pigs fiasco.

When Allen Dulles died in 1969, Prescott wrote a letter of condolence to Dulles' wife Clover. The letter discussed the time after the Bay of Pigs when Allen confided in Prescott that Kennedy would be replacing him as head of the CIA with John McCone. That incident enraged Prescott, and it turned Kennedy into an enemy of his. The letter read:

> He tried to make a pleasant evening of it, but I was rather sick of heart, and angry too, for it was the Kennedys that brought about the fiasco. And here they were making Allen to be the goat, which he wasn't and did not deserve. I have never forgiven them. Well maybe

---

86 James A. Warren, Did CIA Director Allen Dulles Order the Hit on JFK? (The Daily Beast, 2015) http://www.thedailybeast.com/articles/2015/10/13/did-allen-dulles-order-the-hit-on-jfk.html

it was time for him to step down anyway so we shall not dwell on it, but they did make me mad.[87]

The fact that Prescott wrote that he never forgave the Kennedys is particularly disturbing, considering that John F. Kennedy was killed five years before the letter was written and Robert F. Kennedy was killed six months before the letter was sent. Bush served in the Senate with Kennedy and backed Richard Nixon, one of his proteges in the 1960 election.

While Prescott Bush may have been at odds with the Kennedys, he was a good friend with Lyndon Johnson. Despite the fact that Lyndon Johnson was a Democrat they were very close and mutual admirers. According to George H.W. Bush's daughter, Dorothy, Johnson told George H.W. that his father, Prescott, was the best thing that happened to the 83rd congress. Both Bushes, Prescott and George H.W., were close with Lyndon Johnson.

When Lyndon Johnson left office in 1969, he told George H.W. Bush, "Please know that I value your friendship as I do your father's, and that I am glad you are one of us down in Texas." In 1970, Johnson supported George H.W.'s campaign for Senator of Texas, as would President Nixon. After losing the election, Bush then served as Nixon's ambassador to the United Nations.

While political parties may have separated the Bushes and Lyndon Johnson, they were united by friendship and a mutual interest in the Texas oil industries. Texas oil millionaires funded Johnson, including Clint Murchison, Sid Richardson, and Haroldson L.(HL) Hunt. Bush was also close with HL Hunt and Hunt's son helped run George H.W. Bush's 1970 campaign.

---

87 Kitty Kelley, *The Family: The Real Story Of The Bush Dynasty* (Doubleday, 2004) 185

Lyndon Johnson named Prescott Bush's best friend, Allen Dulles to the Warren Commission, the same person who Kennedy forced out as CIA director. Gerald Ford, who would go on to name George H.W. Bush the CIA director as President, would also be named to the Warren Commission by Johnson.

With the many allegations and admissions of CIA involvement in the JFK assassination, the fact that Dulles was named to investigate the murder of Kennedy screams of a cover up. Like Prescott Bush, CIA agents kept their loyalty to Dulles after the Bay Of Pigs while blaming Kennedy for its failure.

Many believe in order for the CIA's role of the assassination to be covered up, the President, Warren Commission, FBI and several key politicians had to be involved. The one man who could tie them together was Prescott Bush. Bush was close to Lyndon Johnson, Allen Dulles, and Richard Nixon, all who were involved with the cover up, if not the conspiracy, to kill Kennedy.

The assassination was, in effect, a coup d'etat, with Kennedy being replaced by Johnson, which required the backing of the CIA, the FBI, and several rich and powerful people. Prescott Bush has to be an ideal suspect as the mastermind of the coup. He was connected to Allen Dulles, who had the loyalty of the CIA, who organized the killing, and to Lyndon Johnson and Richard Nixon, the men who replaced Kennedy and covered it up.

The Kennedy assassination and cover up and the large amount of Skull and Bones members in the CIA and connected to it, are once again tied to the secret team. The CIA and the Mafia may have been used to kill Kennedy, but it would have to take someone with a lot of power and connections to cover up the killing and hide the conspiracy.

The CIA agents who were involved in the Kennedy killing were clearly not loyal to the president, but who were they loyal to? The CIA men alleged to be involved in the conspiracy, E. Howard Hunt, Frank Sturgis, David Atlee Phillips, Cord Meyer, and James Angleton, were all loyal to the CIA Director Allen Dulles.

When Kennedy fired Dulles and threatened to break the CIA into a thousand pieces he made an enemy out of the CIA, a group that was trained to assassinate foreign leaders and then cover it up. It's certainly plausible that Lyndon Johnson, Prescott Bush's good friend, was in on the conspiracy and the cover up. Johnson appointed Dulles onto the Warren Commission, in charge of investigating the JFK killing. This gave the spymaster Dulles a chance to cover up the work of his own men.

Nixon, a protege of Prescott Bush, also was involved in the cover up of the JFK assassination, which would become his downfall through Watergate. Nixon's Vice President and successor, Gerald Ford, was also on the Warren Commission that covered up the CIA's role in the murder of an American president.

I believe the secret team killed Kennedy because he dared to cross Allen Dulles and the CIA. After the Cuban Missile crisis, Kennedy was seen as being weak on Communism, and his reluctance to escalate the Vietnam War angered many hawks on the right. The powers behind the assassination may never be revealed but we can be sure that the Johnson, Nixon, and Ford administrations were all involved with the conspiracy. The secret team would return to power when Prescott Bush's son George H.W. Bush became Vice President in 1980, four years after serving under Ford as Director of the CIA.

Prescott Bush, Allen Dulles, Richard Nixon, Lyndon Johnson, and Gerald Ford represent the political wing of the secret team. The Skull and Bones secret society of Yale University is just one unifying thread between the powerful businessmen, the politicians, and the CIA. The team that pulled off the Kennedy coup and assassination was comprised of CIA agents, businessmen, politicians, and the Mafia.

The politicians behind the Kennedy coup managed to run the country for 14 years after the JFK assassination with LBJ, Nixon, and Ford, and then another 12 years under Reagan and Bush. Porter Goss, another Yale CIA man with ties to Operation 40, became George W. Bush's Director of the CIA in 2004. This secret team would be the driving force in the war against Communism. Ironically, this war included drugs and terrorism, two things that the American government would also declare war on.

CHAPTER 18

George Bush of the CIA

To understand the type of organization the CIA was in 1976, you must understand its leader. George H.W. Bush was not the outsider to the CIA that he claimed he was in 1976 just before he was appointed as director of the agency. His ties to the CIA through family, friends, and college run extremely deep. All indications point to the fact that Bush was involved in a secret team of CIA and other government officials that was involved in the Bay of Pigs, the Kennedy assassination, Watergate, and later, the Iran-Contra scandal.

Zapata Oil, a company founded by Bush in 1953, was by all accounts a front for the CIA. One of Bush's partners in Zapata Oil was Thomas J. Devine. Devine was a CIA agent who left the CIA in 1953, the same year Zapata Oil was founded. Devine officially rejoined the CIA in 1963, working as a witting commercial asset for the CIA's WUBRINY program. Devine worked in Haiti with Lee Harvey Oswald's close friend and alleged CIA handler, George de Mohrenschildt.[88]

Devine continued a close friendship and working relationship with Bush after he left Zapata Oil. Devine accompanied Bush, then a congressman, to Vietnam in 1967. Devine was given top-

---

88 Joan Mellen, Our Man in Haiti: *George de Mohrenschildt and the CIA in the Nightmare Republic* (Trine Day, 2012)

secret clearance from the defense department and CIA on his trips with Bush while still working for the CIA.

Another co-founder of Zapata Oil was Bill Liedtke. Nixon appointed Liedtke as the Texas finance chairman for his presidential campaign. When Zapata later merged with Pennzoil, Liedtke became president of the company. Liedtke also raised money for Nixon's infamous Committee for the Re-Election of the President, which included the Watergate scandal figure G. Gordon Liddy and E. Howard Hunt, the former CIA agent who later admitted to being involved in the plot to kill JFK. The money would be laundered through Mexico in what they called a slush fund through a CIA pipeline. It would be given to the former CIA agents who were involved in the Bay of Pigs and Watergate as hush money to keep them quiet about their activities.

There are several pieces of evidence that point to George Bush being part of the CIA's Bay of Pigs failed invasion. *Barron's Magazine* called Zapata Oil, Bush's company, a part time purchasing front for the CIA. The code name of the Bay of Pigs was Operation Zapata, as was the area in Cuba where the Bay of Pigs was launched from. Two ships used in the Bay of Pigs invasion were named the Barbara J and the Houston, the names of Bush's wife and the city he worked and lived in.

Both Fidel Castro and Cuban Counter Intelligence Chief Fabian Escalante have claimed that Bush was involved in the CIA assassination and the terrorist program Operation 40. Escalante claimed that Bush would assemble businessmen for the Texas Oil industry to fund Operation 40.[89]

---

89 Russ Baker, *Family of Secrets: The Bush Dynasty, America's Invisible Government, and the Hidden History of the Last Fifty Years* (Bloomsbury Press, 2008) 83.

According to William Corson, a former Marine intelligence worker, Bush was an ideal recruiter for the CIA. U.S. Army Brigadier General Russell Bowen[90] and former CIA agent John Sherwood would also claim that Bush was a CIA agent working with anti-Castro Operations in the early 60s[91].

Bush stayed connected to the infamous Operation 40 unit for his whole career, from trying to protect the Watergate burglar and Operation 40 veteran Frank Sturgis, to appointing Operation 40 veteran Ted Shackley as his second in command while director of the CIA. Later, as Vice President, Bush worked closely with Felix Rodriguez, another CIA agent who worked with Operation 40, during the Iran-Contra affair, along with Operation 40's most infamous terrorist, Luis Posada Carrilles. He also would be tied to Barry Seal, a pilot for Operation 40 by several journalists and authors. Bush would pardon another terrorist from Operation 40, Orlando Bosch, when he was President in 1990. Bush's son, George W. Bush, would appoint another Operation 40 member, Porter Goss, as head of the CIA.

Like many of the members of Operation 40, Bush was implicated in the assassination of John F. Kennedy. A memo from J. Edgar Hoover shortly after the JFK assassination had a George Bush of the Central Intelligence Agency relaying a message to the FBI about anti-Castro Cubans planning to take an unauthorized raid on Cuba after the JFK assassination[92]. Given that many CIA trained Anti-Castro Cubans have been implicated

---

90 Richard Belzer, David Wayne *Hit List: An In-Depth Investigation into the Mysterious Deaths of Witnesses to the JFK Assassination* (Skyhorse Publishing)

91 Joseph Trento, *Prelude to Terror: Edwin P. Wilson and the Legacy of America's Private Intelligence Network* (Basic Books, 2006) 17.

92 Associated Press, '63 F.B.I. Memo Ties Bush to Intelligence Agency (The New York Times, 1988) http://www.nytimes.com/1988/07/11/us/63-fbi-memo-ties-bush-to-intelligence-agency.html

in JFK's murder, the fact that Bush was in close contact with them implicates him as well.

There was another government memo from George Bush dealing with the JFK assassination, warning of a James Parrott who Bush had heard was planning to kill Kennedy.[93] Parrott had nothing to do with the assassination by any accounts, leading one to believe it was to distract investigators from the real culprits, the CIA with whom he was working for according to the other memo.

Bush's connection to the JFK assassination does not end with his connections to the CIA, his father, Skull and Bones, Operation 40, and the two memos. A close associate of Bush was George de Mohrenschildt, a man connected to both Texas oil companies and the CIA, but also very close with Lee Harvey Oswald, the patsy and fall guy in the JFK assassination.

George de Mohrenschildt worked as a businessman in Haiti and Latin America, where he did business with the CIA. He would help Oswald get set up with housing and employment in Dallas, before leaving for Haiti before Oswald would be arrested for JFK's murder.

After the Kennedy murder, de Mohrenschildt testified to the Warren Commission about his relationship with Oswald, giving the longest interview of anyone involved. After leaving Haiti, de Mohrenschildt wound up being a teacher at Bishop College and would write letters to Bush asking for money, signing them, "your old friend, G. De Mohrenschildt."

In 1976, Bush received another letter from de Mohrenschildt under more chilling circumstances. De Mohrenschildt had begun to write about his friendship with Lee Harvey Oswald

---

93 Affidavit Of George William Bush http://aarclibrary.org/notices/Affidavit_of_George_William_Bush_880921.pdf

and believed that the CIA and the Mafia were persecuting him for it. He wrote the then-director of the CIA:

> You will excuse this hand-written letter. Maybe you will be able to bring a solution to the hopeless situation I find myself in. My wife and I find ourselves surrounded by some vigilantes; our phone bugged; and we are being followed everywhere. Either FBI is involved in this or they do not want to accept my complaints. We are driven to insanity by the situation. I have been behaving like a damn fool ever since my daughter Nadya died from [cystic fibrosis] over three years ago. I tried to write, stupidly and unsuccessfully, about Lee H Oswald and must have angered a lot of people I do not know. But to punish an elderly man like myself and my highly nervous and sick wife is really too much. Could you do something to remove the net around us? This will be my last request for help and I will not annoy you any more. Good luck in your important job. Thank you so much.[94]

This letter clearly shows de Mohrenschildt believed government forces affiliated with Bush were behind the surveillance and harassment of him because of his writings about Oswald and the Kennedy assassination. He later told journalist Willem Oltmans that he was a middle man between Lee Harvey Oswald and Texas oil tycoon HL Hunt in an assassination plot between Texas oil men, anti-Castro Cubans, the FBI, and the CIA.

Bush would reply to de Mohrenschildt's letter in an apologetic yet secretive tone:

---

94 Russ Baker, *Family of Secrets: The Bush Dynasty, America's Invisible Government, and the Hidden History of the Last Fifty Years* (Bloomsbury Press, 2008) 268.

Let me say first that I know it must have been difficult for you to seek my help in the situation outlined in your letter. I believe I can appreciate your state of mind in view of your daughter's tragic death a few years ago, and the current poor state of your wife's health. I was extremely sorry to hear of these circumstances. In your situation I can well imagine how the attentions you described in your letter affect both you and your wife. However, my staff has been unable to find any indication of interest in your activities on the part of Federal authorities in recent years. The flurry of interest that attended your testimony before the Warren Commission has long subsided, I can only speculate that you may have become "newsworthy" again in view of the renewed interest in the Kennedy assassination, and thus may be attracting the attention of people in the media. I hope this letter had been of some comfort to you, George, although I realize I am unable to answer your question completely.[95]

A few months after Bush sent the letter, de Mohrenschildt was found dead of shotgun wounds, in what authorities said was suicide. Before he was killed, he had started talking to journalists about the JFK assassination and was visited by Gaeton Fonzi of the House Select Committee on Assassinations who left his business card at his house.

Another close partner of George H.W. Bush's was Robert Gow. Gow was another Bush crony whose pedigree and career closely fit that of a CIA agent. A Yale and Skull and Bones man who had worked for Bush at Zapata Oil, Gow went on to run

---

95 Russ Baker, *Family of Secrets: The Bush Dynasty, America's Invisible Government, and the Hidden History of the Last Fifty Years* (Bloomsbury Press, 2008) 269.

a Houston-based agricultural company Stratford, which had several acres of plant nurseries and greenhouses in Jamaica.

Gow later gave George H.W. Bush's son, George W. Bush, a job in his agricultural business in the early 70s. Exactly what CIA-bred Skull and Bones businessmen were doing selling flowers from the Caribbean and Latin America is unclear, but the Skull and Bones clearly had a vested interest in Jamaica.

According to FBI informant Darlene Novinger, the Bush family had close ties to Jamaican drug dealers. In 1982, Novinger infiltrated a drug ring run by the Smatt family, an upper class Lebanese group of brothers in Jamaica, who made their money through rum, tourism, and cocaine.

Novinger claimed that William Smatt, a Jamaican drug lord, would brag about his ties to Bush. Smatt said that he donated money to the Dade County Republican party headed by Bush's son, Jeb, as bribe money for his drug enterprise and that several other drug dealers did the same thing. His brother, Raymond Smatt, claimed that George H.W. Bush and Jeb had done cocaine in his Miami house and that the brothers had provided the Bushes with cocaine and prostitutes.

William Smatt showed Darlene Novinger correspondence, checks, and photographs of himself with the Bush family. He claimed he gave a lot of money to the Bushes and the Republican Party in hopes of being named roaming ambassador for the Bush sponsored Caribbean Basin Initiative, which would provide economic benefits to businessmen such as himself, both legally and illegally.

Darlene Novinger reported she overheard a phone conversation between William Smatt and the Miami Republican Party in which Smatt said, "I just gave you a couple hundred thousand dollars and I want this done!" She would be persecuted her whole life for the allegations she made. Both her husband

and father were killed in suspicious circumstances. Novinger's allegations were never investigated by the FBI and she left the agency.[96]

Another Smatt brother, Ernie, was arrested trying smuggle money out of Jamaica. *The Struggle* magazine claimed the money was intended for Peter Whittingham, the JLP candidate who was charged with planning Operation Werewolf. Whittingham had been arrested in Florida for importing more than two million dollars worth of marijuana into Florida and needed money for a lawyer.

William Smatt went on to write two books. *A Millionaire's Encounter with Cocaine* detailed his experience as a drug addict, without any mention of his alleged drug dealing. *Messiah*, his other book, was about the son of the man he implicated as connected to the drug trade. In *Messiah*, he compared George W. Bush to the second coming of Christ.

Novinger's allegations are consistent with the Bush family's track record of accepting political donations from large-scale narcotics traffickers. Leonel Martinez was a large-scale cocaine and marijuana dealer who was later caught with hundreds of pounds of cocaine. He was also a big contributor to Jeb and George H.W. Bush as well as the Florida Republican party, even managing to take a picture with Vice President Bush. Jeb also had close business ties to several Cuban American businessmen involved in money laundering.[97]

If Novinger's allegations are true, then Bush is guilty of taking money from drug dealers for political favors. This would follow a pattern of both the CIA and the Bush family using the narcotics trade for political gain. Also, if Bush utilized Jamaican

---

96 Rodney Stich, *Drugging America: A Trojan Horse* (Silverpeak, 2008) 419.
97 Jefferson Morley, Dirty Money, (The Miami New Times, 1991) http://www.miaminewtimes.com/news/dirty-money-6365153

drug lords in 1982 as Vice President for political gain, it is not hard to believe that he was utilizing Jamaican drug lords while Director of the CIA in 1976.

Through the years, Bush and his secret team have been guilty of assassinations, narcotics trafficking, terrorism, arms trafficking, and cover-ups. In a meeting with President Ford on June 25, 1976, Bush claimed he was concerned about the charges against the U.S. in Jamaica as well as Cuba. The wars that Bush and the CIA fight are secret dirty wars, funded by drugs, and carried out by assassins and terrorists. This is what Bush brought to Jamaica. Just as the CIA-trained Cubans would go on to become major narco-terrorists, so would the CIA supported anti-Manley Jamaicans after their campaign against Manley in 1976.

CHAPTER 19

THE SECRET TEAM

The CIA and George H.W. Bush's ties to the narco-terrorist Cubans are strong and long. FBI documents show that they have been working with the anti-Castro Cubans since before the JFK assassination. As a part of Operation 40, Bush is at the center of a group that has gone on to be some of the most notorious terrorists, drug dealers, assassins, and CIA agents.

One member of Operation 40 was Felix Rodriguez, who was very close to President George H.W. Bush. They met during his days in the CIA. Both Rodriguez and Posada were also close friends with Watergate burglar Eugenio Martinez, another Operation 40 veteran who was later pardoned by Reagan while Bush was Vice President. Rodriguez was sent to Bolivia by the CIA where he captured and killed Che Guevara, taking his Rolex watch as a souvenir.

Rodriguez later worked for the CIA in Vietnam under Ted Shackley, whom he had previously worked for in the assassination program Operation 40. Shackley was working in Laos with General Vang Pao, who was using money generated from the heroin trade to fund his army against Communist forces. According to author Alfred McCoy, Shackley set up a meeting between old CIA Mafia affiliate Santo Trafficante and Vang Pao to create a drug pipeline from Asia to America that would become known as Air America or by its street name, Air Opium. Retired Marine Colonel Bo Gritz interviewed Burmese ppium warlord Khun Sa, who claimed that Ted Shackley, Santo Trafficante, and Richard Armitage were all partners of his in the opium trade.[98]

Rodriguez worked for the Phoenix program that is said to have been involved in assassinations and torture and the killing of more than 20,000 civilians in Laos and Vietnam.

After returning from Vietnam, Rodriguez set up shop in Miami and partnered up with Gerard Latchinian in the arms business and founded Giro Aviation Corporation. Latchinian would later be arrested by the FBI for plotting to kill the newly elected president of Honduras in 1984. He was convicted of planning a cocaine trade funded coup in Honduras to replace the elected President with a notorious Honduran general.[99]

Rodriguez, Posada, and Bush would team up again in the 80s for what is known as the Iran-Contra scandal. Other Operation 40 veterans involved in Iran-Contra include Ted Shackley, Barry Seal, and Frank Castro who would also take part in the illegal support on the Nicaraguan Contras, often through use of the drug trade. It would seem that the team that got its start in the Bay of Pigs and the JFK assassination continued working with each other in other illegal activities such as drug dealing, assassinations, and terrorism.

Felix Rodriguez was also involved in domestic drug trafficking along with fellow Operation 40 veteran Barry Seal. Seal was a pilot who was used to fly assassins from Operation 40

98 Gyeorgos C. Hatonn, *Threads of Silk - Bands of Steel: Bondage Within the Web* (American West Publishers, 1992) 172.

99 Howard Kohn And Vicki Monks, The Dirty Secrets Of George Bush (Rolling Stone, 1988) http://www.rollingstone.com/politics/news/the-dirty-secrets-of-george-bush-19881103

into Cuba. Like many members of Operation 40, Seal has been connected to the Kennedy assassination. One of Seal's friends later claimed that Seal flew the getaway plane from Dallas after the Kennedy killing.[100] According to CIA pilot Tosh Plumlee, Seal also worked with Rodriguez under Ted Shackley in Laos as a pilot in the in the infamous Air America drug running scheme.

Seal returned from Vietnam only to return to work smuggling arms and explosives to anti-Castro Cubans. In 1972, Seal was arrested for shipping seven tons of C-4 explosives to anti-Castro Cubans in Mexico.[101] After getting off in a mistrial, Seal was released and began a long career as a drug smuggler and informant.

In 1979, Seal was arrested in Honduras with 17 kilos of cocaine, valued at over $2.5 million. He was released after nine months in jail. Soon after, Seal went to work for the Medellin Cartel bringing in cocaine from Colombia through the United States and Nicaragua via an airport located in Mena, Arkansas. Seal used this base to import cocaine from Nicaragua and export guns for the Contras.

After Seal was arrested for smuggling Quaaludes into Florida in 1984, he contacted agents in Vice President George Bush's drug task force. Seal would later be used in a sting operation against Nicaraguan Sandinista forces. Seal provided pictures of a man supposedly connected to the Sandinista forces taking cocaine from Medellin Cartel. After Seal's death, Reagan went on TV using these photos to rally support around the Contras, against the evil drug dealing Sandinistas who were exporting

---

100 Daniel Hopsicker, *Barry and 'the Boys': The CIA, the Mob and America's Secret History* (Trine Day, 2006)

101 Douglas Valentine, *The Strength of the Pack: The Personalities, Politics and Espionage Intrigues that Shaped the DEA* (Trine Day, 2010)

drugs to poison our youth, when in fact, it was the Contras and their CIA supporters who were poisoning the country.

In 1985, an Associated Press article claimed that sources revealed to them that two veterans of the infamous Brigade 2506 group of Bay of Pigs veterans were using armed rebels to guard an airfield in Costa Rica to import cocaine into the Miami area. The article further said that a Nicaraguan Contra leader said a Colombian cartel paid the Contras $50,000 for help with a shipment of 100 kilos of cocaine.

One year after the article was published, Eugene Hasfensus, an Air America veteran, had his plane shot down over Nicaragua. Barry Seal used the same plane on his drugs and arms missions in Central America. When Sandinista forces captured him, he gave up information implicating Max Gomez and Ramon Medina, the aliases of Felix Rodriguez and Luis Posada Carrilles, and a covert air force base in El Salvador that was used to arm the Contras.

According to conservative author R. Emmett Tyrrell, former Bill Clinton bodyguard and Arkansas State Trooper L.D. Brown worked with Barry Seal on his Central American drug missions after Clinton tried to get Brown employment with the CIA. Seal was using the airport in Mena, Arkansas, to import cocaine and export guns to and from Central America. When Brown confronted Clinton about the cocaine being imported in by Seal, Clinton reportedly said, "...that's Lasater's (Clinton's friend, a drug dealer) deal, and your buddy Bush knows all about it."[102]

Brown later met with Felix Rodriguez at the Arkansas governor's mansion. Rodriguez would try and enlist Brown to another CIA operation involving the shipment of arms from the Caribbean to Central America, setting him up at a medical

---

102 R. Emmett Tyrrell, Jr, *Boy Clinton: The Political Biography* (Regnery Publishing, 1996)

school in the island of Montserrat, where he would transport AK-47s and explosives to the Contras.

After Seal was killed by Colombian hitmen in Baton Rouge, Louisiana in 1986, Rodriguez told Brown, "You hear about our man? Well, we know who was flying the second seat." Soon after Rodriguez sent Brown a manual for a gun and directed him to go to Puerto Valla, Mexico, where he was given a gun and directed to kill Seal's partner, Terry Reed. Brown decided against killing Reed and left the CIA and Rodriguez's employment.

In Terry Reed's book *Compromised*, he wrote he had a clash with Felix Rodriguez over the tons of narcotics being shipped from his warehouse and was promised a safe passage out of Mexico if he gave a vow of silence and returned 20 kilos of cocaine. Reed also claimed Bush, Rodriguez, and Oliver North were involved in the illegal cocaine and weapons trade in support of the Contras. According to Reed, Barry Seal was attempting to blackmail George H.W. Bush with information and evidence implicating his sons in cocaine trafficking.[103]

Reed's allegations are backed up by those of Gene Chip Tatum. Tatum worked for Oliver North and with Felix Rodriguez aiding the Contras with medical supplies. The coolers, which were supposed to contain these supplies, were in fact hundreds of kilos of cocaine, which were flown into the infamous airport in Mena, Arkansas.

Tatum worked closely with Barry Seal who would boast about having information that would implicate Vice President Bush in Oliver North's cocaine enterprise. Seal would give Tatum a list of government officials involved in the drug trade that included Felix Rodriguez, Oliver North, and George H.W. Bush along with Israeli Mossad agent Michael Harari, Panamanian dictator

---

103 Terry Reed And John Cummings, *Compromised* (S.P.I. Books, 1994))

Manuel Noriega, Jorge Luis Ochoa Vasquez, and Carlos Lehder of the Medellin Cartel, and several Nicaraguan Contra leaders. Tatum would also claim that Barry Seal had video evidence implicating George H.W. Bush's sons, Jeb and George W., in the cocaine trade.[104]

According to Ramon Milian Rodriguez, an accountant who laundered billions of dollars for Pablo Escobar and the Medellin Cartel and cocaine smuggler and Panamanian President Manuel Noriega, Felix Rodriguez solicited him for money, totaling more than $10 million, to fund the Contra rebels in Nicaragua. In return the government would drop money laundering charges against Milian Rodriguez. Milian Rodriguez had close ties with Manuel Artime, the leader of Brigade 2506, and one of his first acts as accountant would be paying off the families of the Watergate burglars.[105]

One DEA agent, Celerino Castillo, claimed that while investigating Ilopango airport base in El Salvador, he saw Luis Posada and Felix Rodriguez under the false names Ramon Medina and Max Gomez. Castillo said that Posada and Rodriguez were involved in drug and gun trafficking as well as kidnapping and the training of death squads. When he alerted his superiors, they told him it was a covert operation being run by the White House.[106]

Rodriguez not only worked for the White House, he was close to the Vice President, George H.W. Bush. General John K. Singlaub wrote to Oliver North, concerning Bush's daily conversations with Rodriguez.

---

104 Chip Tatum, The Tatum Chronicles, http://www.whale.to/b/tatum.pdf

105 Guns Drugs And The CIA (Frontline, PBS) http://www.pbs.org/wgbh/pages/frontline/shows/drugs/archive/gunsdrugscia.html

106 Celerino III Castillo And Dave Harmon, *Powderburns: Cocaine, Contras & the Drug War* (Mosaic Press, 2010)

According to notes, Assistant Secretary of State Elliot Abrams told Secretary of State George P. Schultz.

> Felix Rodrigues [sic] Bush did know him from CIA days. FR [Rodriguez] is ex-CIA. In El Salv[ador] he goes around to bars saying he is buddy of Bush. A y[ea]r ago Pdx [Poindexter] & Ollie [North] told VP staff stop protecting FR as a friend we want to get rid of him from his involemevnt [sic] w[ith] private ops. Nothing was done so he still is there shooting his mouth off.[107]

It is unlikely that the CIA days Abrams was referring to was Bush's brief tenure as director in 1976, as Rodriguez had retired from the CIA in early 1976. It is most likely that Abrams was referring to Bush and Rodriguez's relationship going back to the 1960s and Operation 40 as previous government memos have shown. Rodriguez has a picture of himself and Bush on his wall at home and has received letters and Christmas cards from Bush. In interviews, he wears a tiepin given to him by the CIA director turned President.

When Bush became CIA director in 1976, he was far from a newcomer at the CIA. In fact, he had been part of a CIA-based secret team of individuals who were involved in the Bay of Pigs, the JFK assassination, the Air America opium smuggling, Watergate, and Iran-Contra. Under Bush as CIA director, the secret team went on a terrorism and assassination spree against any country that would dare have friendly relations with Cuba.

Aside from Bush's close relationship with Ted Shackley, who by many accounts masterminded the secret opium-funded war in Laos, Bush also worked closely with Donald Gregg. Gregg

---

107 Walsh Iran/Contra Report Chapter 29 https://fas.org/irp/offdocs/walsh/chap_29.htm

worked alongside both Shackley and Rodriguez in Laos and Vietnam and later worked with those same people in the drug funded illegal war in Nicaragua that led to the Iran-Contra affair.

Gregg, who became Vice President Bush's National Security advisor, was a CIA officer with a long history with the agency's anti-Castro Cubans. According to authors Webster Griffin Tarpley and Anton Chaitkin, Donald Gregg was the man who recruited both Luis Posada and Felix Rodriguez for Operation 40.[108] Gregg reunited with Bush and Rodriguez to arm the Nicaraguan Contras in the 80s. Felix Rodriguez brought another Operation 40 veteran, Luis Posada, into the mix after he had broken out of a Venezuelan prison, where he was incarcerated for organizing an airline bombing that killed 73 people.

Other members of Bush's secret team included Edwin Wilson, Thomas Clines, Frank Terpil, and General Richard Secord. Edwin Wilson, like many CIA agents, would go into the arms business after leaving the agency in 1971 while still working with the CIA. After his retirement, Wilson would still work closely with Thomas Clines and Ted Shackley who remained in the CIA, working for George H.W. Bush.

Wilson was questioned in the assassination of Orlando Letelier and charged with hiring anti-Castro Cuban Operation 40 veteran Rafael Quintero to assassinate an enemy of Libyan leader Muammar Gaddafi in Egypt. While Wilson was found not guilty of the assassination charge, he was found guilty of selling weapons and over 20 tons of C-4 explosives to the Libyan government. During his trial in 1984, he defended himself by saying he was working with the CIA. The CIA would deny his involvement but after he served 22 years in prison, his conviction was overturned after a judge found out that he in fact

---

108 Webster Griffin Tarpley And Anton Chaitkin, *George Bush: The Unauthorized Biography* (Progressive Press, 2004)

was working with the CIA.[109] Wilson would work with another ex-CIA agent, Frank Terpil, who would become the right hand man to brutal Ugandan dictator Idi Amin.

Though Thomas Clines left the CIA in 1978, he, too, would remain a part of the secret team of George H.W. Bush. Clines was involved in the CIA's anti-Castro efforts in Miami in the 60s. He worked with several of the people implicated in the Kennedy assassination, including David Atlee Phillips and David Sanchez Morales. Clines worked under Ted Shackley, who he would follow to Laos where they implemented an opium-funded secret illegal war, where thousands of innocent people were killed.

Clines continued to work with Shackley under George H.W. Bush in 1976, rising to the number three man in the agency. In 1978, he left the agency and teamed up with fellow former CIA agents Ted Shackley and Edwin Wilson to form API distributors. Many CIA agents after leaving the agency use their training and contacts from the CIA to go into the weapons trade, often while still working closely with the CIA.

Gene Wheaton, who worked closely with the CIA, claimed Shackley and Clines were running a top-secret assassination program dating back to the early 60s. According to Wheaton, the assassination program also included anti-Castro Cubans Felix Rodriguez and Rafael Quintero. Quintero was another Operation 40 veteran who would follow Shackley to Laos for his

---

109 Douglas Martin, Edwin P. Wilson, the Spy Who Lived It Up, Dies at 84 (The New York Times, 2012) http://www.nytimes.com/2012/09/23/us/edwin-p-wilson-cia-operative-with-cloak-and-dagger-life-dies-at-84.html?_r=0

opium-funded secret war. Wheaton later claimed that Quintero was involved in the JFK assassination.[110]

One of the men Quintero hired for assassinations for Edwin Wilson and Thomas Clines, was Rafael Villaverde. Rafael was yet another Bay of Pigs veteran who got caught up in the narcotics and assassinations trade. In 1982, he was charged with running a multi-million dollar cocaine ring but would disappear before facing trial. Another man implicated in the same cocaine ring was Frank Castro, the CIA-trained narco-terrorist who would work with Orlando Bosch and Luis Posada in CORU's 1976 international anti-Castro terror campaign. According to Frank Terpil, both Ted Shackley and Thomas Clines were also involved in the same cocaine ring.

Another former CIA agent, Bradley Ayers, said that Shackley, Rodriguez, and Clines all had "intimate operational knowledge" of the JFK assassination.[111] The former CIA agents Shackley, Clines, and Rodriguez continued their illegal operations under George H.W. Bush twenty years after the JFK assassination, in what would wind up as the Iran-Contra scandal.

Ted Shackley and Thomas Clines also worked with Iranian arms dealer Albert Hakim selling arms to Iran and diverting the profits to provide weapons to the Contras in Nicaragua. In 1990, Clines was sentenced to 16 months in jail for not disclosing the money he made through selling arms to Iran and the Contras to the IRS.

The secret team of Shackley, Clines, and Wilson was also connected to the Nugan Hand Bank in Australia, which was used to launder CIA-connected money from arms and drug

110 David Corn, *Blond Ghost: Ted Shackley and the CIA's Crusades* (Simon & Schuster, 1994)

111 Bradley Ayers, *The Zenith Secret: A CIA Insider Exposes the Secret War Against Cuba and the Plot That Killed the Kennedy Brothers* (Vox Pop, 2007)

trafficking. Former CIA Director Richard Helms called Shackley a triple threat: Drugs, Arms, Money and Murder.

The Bay of Pigs and JFK assassination had given birth to the secret team of CIA agents and the Cubans they trained and commanded; businessmen and politicians united by their cooperation and knowledge of the planned assassination of an American president and its cover-up. Some of these men would go onto Laos where they engaged in drug smuggling and political assassinations. Other members of this group were involved in the Watergate burglary and cover up that would ultimately bring down Richard Nixon.

Ted Shackley was at the center of this secret team, who would also be responsible for the murder of Che Guevara, and the overthrow of the democratically elected president of Chile. Shackley was very close friends with George W. Bush and assisted the Bush/Reagan Presidential campaign in 1980. Shackley's wife, Hazel, who was also a CIA agent, worked for Bush as well. After leaving the CIA, Shackley continued to work with Bush, playing an integral role in the arms for hostages deal with Iran in 1980, during the presidential election.[112] Shackley convinced the Iranian government to postpone the release of American hostages until after the election to ensure Reagan's victory.

When Shackley's close friend and CIA associate William Francis Buckley was kidnapped by Hezbollah in Beirut, Shackley would once again be involved in the trading of arms for hostages with Iran, giving birth to Iran-Contra. The Iran-Contra affair would reunite the same secret team involved in the JFK assassination and the secret drug war in Laos.

---

112 Jonathan Marshall, Peter Dale Scott, Jane Hunter *The Iran-Contra Connection: Secret Teams and Covert Operations in the Reagan Era* (South End Press, 1987) 163.

It seems many people who worked for and with Bush would go on to the drugs, arms, and assassination businesses. In 1976, a good part of the secret team was working for Bush in the CIA. Ted Shackley, Edwin Wilson, and Thomas Clines all took orders from Bush in 1976. Felix Rodriguez and Luis Posada also worked for the CIA in that same year under Bush. The team reunited when Bush became Vice President in the 80s and returned to their habits of involvement in the drug and weapons trade, assassinations, dirty tricks, and cover-ups.

All evidence points to the secret team doing its dirty work in Jamaica in the same manner that they did in Laos and later in Nicaragua, using the drugs and arms trade to empower a pro-American group against their leftist opponents. The drugs, guns, and terrorism that first came to Jamaica in the 70s had all the trademarks of a CIA operation. The secret team's existence in Jamaica at this time would explain a lot of the mysterious events that took place by using their modus operandi to operate like a government-sanctioned Mafia, creating global power through drugs, guns, terrorism, assassination, lies, propaganda and dirty tricks.

CONCLUSION

This book is relevant for several reasons. For people who have read Marlon James' brilliant *A Brief History Of Seven Killings* you may notice several similarities. James' book also dealt with the CIA in Jamaica in the same era by using fiction. Several incidents and characters from his book are based on real life events and people that are covered in my book.

Through fiction, James made several points that are covered in my book as well, that the CIA was responsible for terrorism, gang violence, and the cocaine trade in Jamaica as well as the assassination attempt on Bob Marley.

The events covered in both books are very relevant to what is going on in the world today. While the cold war may be over, CIA interference in international affairs is still a common occurrence. The government of Venezuela has claimed that the CIA and other American groups are behind recent coups and attempts to destabilize their government.

The son of Lester "Jim Brown" Coke, Edward Seaga's bodyguard and cocaine kingpin, Christopher "Dudus" Coke was extradited to the U.S. in 2010 on drug and gun charges. Bruce Golding, who was then-Prime Minister of Jamaica, was reluctant to extradite Coke because he, like his JLP predecessor Edward Seaga who had strong ties to Shower Posse leader Lester Coke, relied on Dudus for support.

Golding would eventually bow to U.S. pressure and used armed forces to invade Tivoli Gardens, the JLP political haven founded by Edward Seaga and birthplace of the Jamaican Shower Posse to capture his former ally. More than seventy residents of Tivoli Gardens were killed in the invasion before Dudus was captured.

If one were to believe the Shower Posse cohorts of Dudus' father Lester, like Cecil Connor (aka Charles "Little Nut" Miller), one would see that Dudus, Tivoli Gardens, and the Shower Posse are all byproducts of the CIA's secret war in Jamaica. By training, arming, and giving the Shower Posse access to the cocaine trade, the CIA helped create a narco-state where the leaders were dependent on drug dealers for support.

Jamaica was caught in the crossfire of two wars: the Cold War and the War on Drugs. The available money from the United States' demand for illegal drugs funded the weapons used by the right wing allies in the Cold War against Communism. What happened in Jamaica and other countries where the CIA took advantage of the drug trade represents the hypocrisy of the War on Drugs. While America is incarcerating Black and Latino men for distributing it at a retail level, its own spy agency, the CIA, is playing a big role in importing it and using the proceeds for their own political agenda.

The result of this hypocritical war on drugs has led to incarcerated black men, black-on-black violence in America and narco-states, and drug money-fueled civil wars in Latin America in the Caribbean. The corporations who make and sell the weapons, who control the private prisons, and exploit Third World countries are the ones who benefit.

Today in Mexico, thousands of people are murdered in drug wars with warring factions fighting for the lucrative proceeds from feeding America's drug habit. Just as Prohibition gave rise to a violent American Mafia, drug prohibition has fueled the Mexican cartels with American money and weapons.

In the book I've presented a plethora of evidence and allegations about the CIA, both in Jamaica and the world. I wrote about the CIA's involvement in the secret war against Castro, the JFK assassination, and involvement in the drug trade to paint a picture of the organization, its capabilities, and its philosophy that were applied to Jamaica.

I believe the CIA does not represent the United States and that if Americans knew what the CIA really has done and continued to do, they would call for an end to the agency. That's why the CIA is so secretive. In truth, the CIA does not represent the interests of the American people but select American businesses, individuals, and select right-wing politicians. We may never know the whole story about what the CIA was doing in Jamaica due to the secrecy of the CIA as well as the Jamaican politicians and criminals they worked with.

Still, there are several pieces of evidence that point directly to CIA being involved in a plan to undermine the Manley regime. The smoking gun is the plane that Luis Posada and Orlando Bosch destroyed by a bomb on the way to Jamaica from Barbados in October of 1976, killing 73 people, which was the same plane that was targeted for bombing by the same group in Jamaica a few months earlier. The CIA-trained Cubans, led by Posada, went on a terror spree in the Caribbean that year, in a calculated attempt to deter any country in the region from having friendly relations with Cuba.

Manley had an informant in Miami that directly tied the terrorism in Jamaica to the anti-Castro Cuban exiles who have long acted as the gangster wing of the CIA engaging in the dirty work of assassinations, terrorism, and drug dealing.

It is hard to separate Posada from the CIA and it is not clear if his actions came with the direction or just the protection of the CIA. As Director of the CIA, Vice President, and President, George H.W. Bush has protected Bosch and Posada. It is hard to believe that Posada ever stopped working for the CIA. After breaking out prison in Venezuela, he would go right back to working for Bush's friend Felix Rodriguez in the cocaine and weapons business in El Salvador.

Despite that as CIA Director, Bush would have been fully aware of the terrorist activities by Orlando Bosch, he pardoned and released Bosch in 1990 when he returned to Miami after decades of committing acts of terrorism. Posada, too, would be free after returning to the United States in 2007, this time under Bush's son, and was set free by a Texas judge who happened to be appointed by George W. Bush.

Michael Manley's allegations against the CIA must be taken seriously. While some claim that Manley was making a scapegoat of the CIA in order to win the election, it is clear Manley believed there was a CIA plot against him. The terrorism that happened in January of 1976 during the IMF and the seemingly coordinated violence that came after it, followed by negative reports in the international press had all the makings of a CIA effort.

The reasons for Manley's State of Emergency remain unclear to this day. He had wanted to declare a State of Emergency after the IMF riots but was deterred by the Army to do so. To this day, the JLP will claim that Manley used the State of Emergency as a political ploy and the matter was even taken up in court.

The strange case of Albert "Spy" Robinson and the arrests of JLP politicians Pearnel Charles and Peter Whittingham for the alleged plot to overthrow the government may never be fully understood. What we do know is that the American Embassy feared that the whole situation would look bad for them and their assets in the Jamaican government.

The cables from Ambassador Gerard indicate that Michael Manley had information that would discredit the American government. Manley's informants in Miami had given him information on the alleged plot to overthrow the government that lead to the State of Emergency as well as information on the anti-Castro Cubans who bombed the plane in Jamaica.

These cables also show Manley possibly had further information to discredit the CIA and U.S. involvement in Jamaica that he never brought up. As the year 1976 came to an end, Manley and the PNP toned down their critiques of the CIA and their connection to the JLP and plan to destabilize Jamaica.

The reasons for this are clear. Manley realized the difference between the United States and the CIA, who he believed often acted as a rogue agency. Manley did not want to create tension with the U.S., but he did want the CIA out of Jamaica for good. Manley was hoping for a change in U.S.-Jamaican relations and knew that 1976 was an election year in the U.S. as well.

The American government in power in 1976 was the remnant of the old corrupt Nixon regime, plagued by the Watergate scandal. Gerald Ford, Nixon's former Vice President was President, Henry Kissinger, who was Nixon's Secretary of State, remained so under Ford. Dick Cheney was Chief of Staff, Donald Rumsfeld was Secretary of Defense, and, of course, George H.W. Bush was the director of the CIA.

Manley was hoping that progressive Democrat Jimmy Carter would defeat Ford in the 1976 election which would lead to better relations between the United States and Manley's progressive social democratic government. Gerard, the U.S. Ambassador to Jamaica, received information that Manley had stopped his criticism of the CIA in the hopes of getting aid from the newly elected Carter administration. Manley called for elections in Jamaica a month after Carter was elected in the United States.

If Manley had really wanted to discredit the CIA, he had all the ammunition he wanted. Manley was aware of the former and current CIA agents who were involved in the bombing the Cubana flight 455 at the airport named after his father Norman Manley, in July of 1976. Fidel Castro blamed the CIA when the same plane was bombed in October of the same year, killing 73 civilians while Manley would be quiet on the issue.

Manley was hoping that he could be a go-between for both Cuba and the U.S. to improve relations between the countries. In the short-term, Manley was able to defeat the CIA and win the election but would wind up losing the next election in 1980, in what would be a low intensity civil war. The forces trained and armed by the CIA wound up defeating Manley with assistance from the economic sabotage that left Jamaica in poverty.

Unlike in the cases of Watergate and Iran-Contra where a burglary arrest and an American plane shot down lead to two big investigations and scandals, in Jamaica there was never any media or government investigations into the CIA involvement in Jamaica.

The few media investigations of CIA in Jamaica came from *Counterspy* magazine in 1976, "CIA And Local Gunmen Plan Jamaica Coup", and *Penthouse's* article "Murder As Usual" in 1977. Though a magazine known more for naked women than hard-hitting investigations, the *Penthouse* article was taken seriously enough that the CIA publicly attacked the article. The journalists who wrote the *Penthouse* story, Ernest Volkman and John Cummings, both have gone on to write several other books relating to spying and organized crime and, by all accounts, are respected, credible journalists.

Counterspy was sued by the CIA for revealing the identities of CIA agents and was well known in the intelligence community for its accurate reporting on the CIA. The magazine was founded by ex-CIA agent Philip Agee, a man who was a thorn in the side of the agency for years. Agee's visit to Jamaica was a major event that the American Embassy believed discredited the CIA and helped Michael Manley win the election a few months later.

Agee was later accused by George H.W. Bush of providing information that led to the murder of a CIA agent, and these actions led to the Intelligence Identities Protection Act that made naming a CIA agent illegal.

Agee may be discredited for his politics and affiliation with the KGB and Cuban intelligence, but America can not discredit the truth to his claims. In his September visit to Jamaica, Agee provided information and named several CIA agents working out of the American Embassy. Many of these former Embassy officials have since proclaimed that they were CIA agents and have it on their resume and talk about their experiences openly.

Agee is a credible source of information on the philosophy and actions of the CIA. It is doubtful we would have come to Jamaica if the CIA did not have a strong presence there. By naming names and showing patterns of CIA behavior that was in Jamaica, the CIA and the U.S. clearly took Agee's allegations seriously according to cables from the ambassador.

The Marley shooting is a mystery that has not been solved in nearly 40 years. Like the JFK assassination, there are many theories and many alleged culprits. Also like the JFK assassination, most of those theories involve the CIA.

Other theories say the PNP organized the hit on Marley. It is hard to believe that Manley would try and have Marley killed, right before a concert that was seen as a PNP rally and after he

. Bob and Michael Manley would reason with each other and Marley was a great provider for Jamaica.

Further, if the JLP or some of their armed gunmen were involved, it is likely they got their orders from the CIA. While the JLP would benefit from Marley not performing at the Smile Jamaica concert, Marley provided for families and was close friends with gangsters from both political parties. Marley was not attacking the JLP in his music and his support of the PNP was not blatant or obvious other than the Smile Jamaica concert.

It would seem that the CIA would be the group most likely to want to have Marley killed. Marley had called the CIA out by name, not the JLP or the PNP. The CIA would risk losing the election in Jamaica in order to have Marley killed. Marley's voice had become a global one, urging people everywhere to stand up against oppressive regimes, many who were supported by the CIA.

Many experts and historians on Jamaica, reggae music, and Bob Marley believe the CIA was behind the Marley shooting, including reggae archivist Roger Steffens, Marley biographer Timothy White, author Laurie Gunst, and music journalists Chris Farley and Chris Salewicz . Their theories are backed up by Don Taylor's story of the assassin confessing that he was paid in guns and cocaine to shoot Marley.

The evolution of the guns and drugs trade, and the murderous gangsters and corruption that comes with it in Jamaica has all the markings of the CIA. The agency has long used the narcotics trade and organized crime in its battles against Communism and Jamaica would seem to be no different.

Organized crime and the narcotics trade play a big part in history but have few historical records. The fact there is no paper trail for drug transactions makes it an ideal way for the

CIA to fund armed groups covertly without the knowledge of the media or Congress.

The CIA's long history of employing and working with drug dealers such as Laotian General Vang Pao, Florida Mafia drug kingpin Santo Trafficante, and Panamanian dictator Manuel Noriega have a pattern forming a modus operandi for the organization. The large numbers of Cubans trained by the CIA that went on to become big players in the cocaine trade either after or during the career's with the agency strengthen the ties between the CIA and the narcotics trade.

Jamaica itself is an ideal point for the cocaine trade with its location right in between the cocaine producers in South America and the consumers in the United States. Seaga's stronghold of Tivoli Gardens borders the port in Jamaica giving the area access to guns and drugs that come in from the United States and South America.

When Castro took over Cuba, the Mafia lost not only a major source of revenue from the casinos, but also a major narcotics and weapons transshipment center. The CIA-connected mafia drug kingpin Santo Trafficante would have to relocate drug trafficking operations from Cuba to other countries in Latin America in order in order to keep up the Mafia supply of narcotics in the 60s and 70s. Many Cubans involved in Trafficante's drug smuggling organization would go on to work for the CIA as well.

According to several sources, Trafficante continued his connection with the CIA in the drug trade after the failed plots against Castro. Trafficante worked with CIA agent Ted Shackley in Laos, bringing opium from Asia to the United States. After the Vietnam War ended, so did the pipeline for heroin from Asia.

During the 1970s, as cocaine became more popular in elite crowds and discos, the demand for cocaine in America rose. Not only was Jamaica an ideal location for the cocaine trade, but Jamaicans had a history of smuggling marijuana into the United States making Jamaica an ideal pipeline for the narcotics trade.

Michael Manley warned of a Mafia plot to turn Jamaica to a hub for hard drugs, which he connected to a greater U.S. destabilization plot. The Mafia he was referring to was Santo Trafficante's narcotics trafficking organization of CIA-trained Cubans. These Cubans seized control of the cocaine trade aided by their Latin American and Mafia contacts.

In the late 70s and early 80s, there seems to be a pattern of cocaine-funded right-wing governments and rebel groups in the Caribbean and Latin America. The CIA sponsored dictators like Manuel Noriega, Augusto Pinochet, and Contra leader Danilo Blandon.

A common thread between CIA drug trafficking and Latin American dictators are the anti-Castro Cubans, trained by the Americans, who branched out to help right-wing dictatorships all over South America. Under Operation Condor, right-wing military dictatorships in South America would undertake a campaign of silencing opponents through kidnapping, torture, and assassinations. Several CIA-trained Cubans, such as Luis Posada, assisted in these operations through agencies like the Chilean DINA.

As cocaine became the biggest export for several Latin American countries, the CIA realized that controlling the cocaine trade was the best way to control Latin America. For the agency a right-wing military cocaine funded dictatorship was better than a leftist democratically elected government. In 1978, there was a right-wing coup in Honduras funded by cocaine dealers, and in 1980, cocaine traffickers would also finance a coup in Bolivia. These military takeovers would become known as cocaine coups that had the full support of the CIA. The players and patterns in Jamaica had all the markings of a CIA cocaine operation. While not a military dictator or armed rebel leader, Seaga had control of a small armed militia. The cocaine exporting and weapons increased dramatically after Jamaica became a major target of the CIA in 1976.

In the 1980s, Jamaica evolved into a major transshipment point for cocaine along with Honduras, El Salvador, and Costa Rica, three countries in which CIA-trained Cubans controlled narcotics operations to fund the Contras. Panama, under CIA asset Manuel Noriega, became a prime location for cocaine smuggling and money laundering. Testimony from Michael Vogel to the Kerry Committee paints Jamaica in the 1980s as a place where drugs traveled freely without government interest and Seaga as a man reaping the benefits of the drug trade in his country.

With all of the patterns and evidence of a CIA narco-trafficking effort in Jamaica, we must seriously consider the allegations of members of the Shower Posse, the gang that often served as the armed, drug trafficking wing of the JLP. Cecil Connor, a high ranking Shower Posse member, claimed the CIA trained him to become the infamous drug lord he would eventually become. Richard "Storyteller" Morrison would also claim that the CIA was involved in his cocaine smuggling between Colombia, Jamaica, and Miami.

Bob Marley's manager, Don Taylor, claimed the CIA paid Jamaican gunmen in guns and cocaine to assassinate Marley is all the more believable after several recent revelations of the CIA's involvement in the cocaine and arms trade. The claim that CIA was arming the JLP come from several sources including Michael Manley, ex-CIA agents John Stockwell and Philip Agee, journalists Ernest Volkman, John Cummings, and Ellen Ray, and authors Laurie Gunst and Gary Webb.

The CIA is a very covert and secretive organization. In many ways, they operate like a government-sanctioned Mafia, with a license to kill and deal drugs and an oath of secrecy to boot. Because the CIA is so secretive, it is hard to tell the full extent of its role in destabilizing Jamaica and the role of the CIA in the drug trade.

In Jamaica, there is enough evidence and many allegations to fit the pattern of the CIA using the drugs and arms trade to further international foreign policy during the Cold War. George H.W. Bush appointed Ted Shackley his second in command while running the CIA. Shackley had previously run Operation Phoenix and its Air America program that imported Laotian heroin to America to fund right-wing General Vang Pao's fight against the Communists.

Bush also used the cocaine trade to further U.S. interests in Central America as Vice President in the 80s. To fund the Contras, Bush facilitated cocaine trafficking from El Salvador, Costa Rica, and Honduras to fund the Contras in Nicaragua. Both Bush and Shackley were part of Secret Team of right-wing politicians, anti-Castro Cubans, narcotic traffickers, Texas oil tycoons, and the Mafia.

This team would get its start in the Bay of Pigs invasion and several plots to kill Castro. When Kennedy failed to support the Bay of Pigs invasion, criticized the CIA for its failure and fired CIA Director Allen Dulles, the team changed its target from Castro to Kennedy.

After the Kennedy assassination, the CIA actively covered up their involvement in the killing by assassinating possible whistleblowers and other dirty tricks. The Watergate Scandal involved the CIA and several anti-Castro Cubans. Today, it is clear that Watergate was an attempt to hide government involvement in the JFK assassination.

In 1976, the secret team was in complete control of the CIA with Bush and Shackley running the show. Under Bush's watch, the anti-Castro Cubans affiliated with his secret team, would go on a terrorism and assassination spree all over Latin America and the Caribbean. These same Cubans were funded by the cocaine trade and protected by the CIA.

Jamaica was just a small part of the CIA's plan for control of third world countries. Through propaganda, economic sabotage, and the weapons and drugs trade, the agency was able to destabilize Jamaica and create a cycle of economic exploitation, narcotics trade, and gun violence that still plagues Jamaica today.

In April of 2015, President Barack Obama visited the Bob Marley Museum at 56 Hope Road in Kingston, the same site where Marley was nearly assassinated. He spoke about the assassination attempt at the University of the West Indies in Jamaica but did not mention the allegations that the CIA was behind it.

Jeb Bush, the son of the CIA Director who presided over its secret war in Jamaica, is running for President in 2016. Hopefully, he will have to defend himself against allegations of involvement in the drug trade during Iran-Contra and support of terrorists like Orlando Bosch and business dealing with anti-Castro Cubans involved in the drug trade.

Recently, 90 pounds of cocaine was found on a boat owned by Republican Senate Majority leader Mitch McConnell's father in law, who also happens to be one of his biggest campaign contributors. McConnell was one of Bush's strongest allies in the Senate during Iran-Contra.

It is evident to me that George H.W. Bush is the clear villain of the story. From his involvement in the Bay of Pigs, JFK assassination, and Watergate to the atrocities and terrorism committed by his Cuban cohorts during his tenure as CIA director in 1976 to Iran-Contra, Bush has been tied to some of the darkest parts of American history and some of its most notorious villains. Bush has had close ties with Felix Rodriguez, Ted Shackley, and other CIA agents who have compromised the secret team. It is more likely that these agents committed acts of narco-trafficking and assassinations on his orders rather than doing so without his knowledge.

I encourage everybody who reads this book to do their own independent research on the actions the CIA has done in Jamaica and elsewhere. We live in a world where information is power and the best way to fight evil doers is to expose their injustices to the world.

~ Casey Gane-McCalla

CASEY GANE-MCCALLA is a journalist and rapper, born in Cambridge, Massachusetts. Born to a South African mother and Jamaican father, he quickly became interested in global politics and history, which he studied at Columbia University. The former staff writer for *NewsOne* has covered a wide variety of subjects from music to politics to drugs and organized crime. *Inside The CIA's Secret War In Jamaica* is his first book, after researching its subject matter for three years. Besides writing, Casey is also involved in music, technology, and filmmaking as a founding partner in the GIF-based music video generator StartUp, MVGEN, the owner of Phoenix Rising Records (distributed by Sony), and the creator of the pioneering hip-hop comedy web series *That's Whats Up*.

YOU CAN FOLLOW THE AUTHOR VIA HIS TWITTER FEED @CASEYGANE.

Lightning Source UK Ltd.
Milton Keynes UK
UKHW012032191119
353844UK00001B/114/P